iving in the
runaway WEST

partisan views from
Writers on the Range

foreword by Timothy Egan
compiled by the Editors
of High Country News

Publisher's Note: All of the essays in *Living in the Runaway West* were written for Writers on the Range, the syndicated columns of *High Country News*, and have been previously published in the same or similar form in various newspapers in the West. The cover and interior photographs originally appeared as part of a photographic feature in *High Country News*.

Library of Congress Cataloging-in-Publication Data

Living in the runaway West : partisan views from writers on the Range / foreword by Timothy Egan ; compiled by the editors of High country news.
        p. cm.
ISBN 1-55591-048-3
1. West (U.S.)—Description and travel—Anecdotes. 2. West (U.S.)—
Social life and customs—20th century—Anecdotes. 3. West (U.S.) Social conditions—20th century—Anecdotes. I. High country news II. Title.
F595.3 .L574 2000
978'.033—dc21   00-009658

Printed in Canada
0 9 8 7 6 5 4 3 2 1

Editorial: Marlene Blessing, Heath Silberfeld
Cover and interior design: Sullivan Santamaria Design Inc.
Cover and interior photos: Steve Collector

Fulcrum Publishing
16100 Table Mountain Parkway, Suite 300
Golden, Colorado 80403
(800) 992-2908 • (303) 277-1623
www.fulcrum-books.com

Contents

153 THE NATURE OF THE WEST—5

197 CULTURE CLASH—6

Foreword

—Timothy Egan

At age eighteen, I had a head full of righteous nonsense, no filter for common sense, and $122 in my pocket as I stood at the on-ramp to Interstate 90 near the Washington–Idaho border. Eastbound, headed for the heart of the West. I had grown tired of our town, bored by the rituals of late adolescence, and was hungry for something greater than the sum of our summer nights. Near dusk on a Friday in early September, a Canadian with a dog strapped into the front seat picked me up and then followed the black road until we were deep in the mountain time zone.

Over the next month, I feasted on the unscripted West. Slept in a churchyard at 9,000 feet, praying to the resident God for dawn to break the hypothermic chill. Talked to ghosts in a mining town three generations past its pull date. In Cody, Wyoming, I fell in love at one end of town, and fell out of love at the other. Saw enough roadkill to feed a cowboy poetry convention. Picked fruit with Mexicans. Inhaled with carny workers. I reveled in all of it, at least in the rearview mirror perspective. And then it was off to college, and a life. But I knew I'd never leave the West.

Now I revisit these places, a man paid to observe and conclude. Some of it, I can't make any sense of. I never have figured out why those people dug caves in Paradise Valley to hide from imminent nuclear apocalypse just as the Cold War was coming to an end. And how did the wildest part of the West produce a woman who hates the wild, Helen Chenoweth, to represent them in Congress? I never go to Montana without coming home with wild huckleberry jam, even at seven dollars for a small jar.

But what I realize, reading this great bundle of essays and thinking about my own beliefs, is how much this place still can surprise me. For too long, the West has been burdened with upholding the national myth, or the countermove to tear it down. Enough already. If you look at it through the eyes of these writers, westerners all, whether they arrived yesterday or can trace their roots to Kennewick Man, what you see is drama without a third act. The Writers on the Range capture the quirks of history, seldom visible to the Big Thinkers.

Sad to say, our national pundits mostly drink from the same pond, near that swamp in the other Washington. The West, to most of them, is flyover country. Oh, sure, every now and then *Time* magazine discovers "A New West" run by dot.com billionaires in mountain-biking togs. Or a lavish seminar in a Rocky Mountain resort will lay out a buffet of the latest corporate wish list disguised as trend-setting protein. And nothing looks sillier than a network news star in a plaid shirt, mistaking a change of scenery for fresh journalism.

At the start of the new century, the West is in the global spotlight, for a number of good reasons. One state, California, will have no ethnic majority within ten years—a polyglot experiment unlike anything the world has ever experienced. And despite the white flight to rural mountain states, hundreds of western counties are seeing similar change. Within a generation, Latinos will comprise nearly 25 percent of the population in many western states that is at the center of the new American demographics. Asian American numbers are growing at four times the national average for other ethnic groups—mostly in the West. And American Indians, revitalized by educated new leaders and money from fresh ventures, are reclaiming lost ground.

So for everyone who wants to write off the West as a Republican monolith, populated by Brady Bunch cul de sacs except for a strip of coastal liberals, look again. The descendants of people who built the railroads, harvested the world's largest agricultural crop, and held tightly to aboriginal ground are now part of a burgeoning western renaissance. It defies traditional politics.

In the public domain—the more than 500 million acres of land that are the birthright of every American—another revival of sorts is underway. After more than a century in which so much of the original American West was all but erased—the wolves killed, the bison wiped out, the major rivers dammed, the old-growth forest stripped bare—a corrective is underway. The timber beasts who used to run the national forests are a dying breed. In a single stroke of the executive pen, a roadless area of nearly 40 million acres—a de facto wilderness larger than any other forest setaside—has just been designated. The federal water agencies that once acted as the orthodontists of nature, trying to straighten every river that flowed crooked and free, now talk of being riparian healers. Wolves are back in the Rockies. Salmon are trying to make a comeback in the Northwest. Even some of the remaining wild grasslands of the prairie are being recognized for their unique value to biodiversity.

But new threats loom. Every hour, an acre of the Sonoran Desert is lost to the sprawl of Greater Phoenix. Salt Lake, Denver, and Seattle have similar appetites. The small towns cling to their Main Streets against the march of Wal-Marts and trophy subdivisions. National treasures face the same peril, as in New Mexico, where plans are moving forward to punch a highway through Petroglyph National Monument. Teachers wonder how to make ends meet in a West that does not look anything like the glossy magazines, and the servant class is anyone who makes less than six figures.

The old extractive industries may be on the run, but the wave of industrial tourism, prophesied by Edward Abbey almost thirty years ago, grows bigger every day. The winter air in Yellowstone National Park is worse than the peak smog of Los Angeles, thanks to snowmobile congestion. Moab has become a metaphor for unsustainable play. And who would have thought a day would ever come when the free-spirit ethic of river rafting would be overcome by take-a-number bureaucracies that mandate drug testing of guides? River rats gave us Tevas, after all, with no help from federal subsidies.

The best stories about all the changes underway in the American West are told by people who are close to the land itself. That is the greatest strength of the Writers on the Range. While reading these essays, I could almost feel the wind blowing through a poorly insulated house, or the stare of a pinch-faced, Gothic politician. Mary Sojourner's image of the middle-aged women in pastel jogging suits silently playing the slots in Nevada is a haunt I will not soon forget.

Some of these stories, in the tradition of Mark Twain's great western travelogue *Roughing It*, are contradictory and ribald. I laughed out loud at Ed Quillen's vision of a New West celebration, no less absurd than an Old West festival built around staged homicide. Dan Dagget takes environmentalists to task for conflict obsession. And here is Rocky Barker, a ferocious journalist who has never been afraid to face down the Old Guard of Idaho, admitting to non-p.c. thoughts as he extols "the smooth action of an old Parker double barrel" in an essay on guns.

Hal Walter's agony over whether to kill a rattlesnake near his subdivision has more to say about predators and their place in the habitat of the West than most book-length tomes on the same subject. And Stephen Lyons asks some very hard questions about race and one-party power in the part of the West that he struggles to continue to love.

The West is too often a fantasy projection: cowboys against the sunset, a picture from a Sierra Club calendar. Yes, it is Wally Stegner's native ground of hope. But it is also a dark place at times, lonely and mean as a Wyoming wind. Accept the West for what it is, and you find it is bittersweet. As old-timers say about Montana weather, "If you don't like it now, wait a minute." The West is most certainly not a static thing, neither sepia-toned nor Kodachrome. These essays are like looking through the viewfinder of a digital camera: capturing a moment fleeting but true to its time.

The Writers on the Range will not threaten the monopoly that usual-suspect pundits still have for interpreting the daily narrative of America. But they have gained a foothold, and in so doing have followed the dictum of poet Gary Snyder. He was asked how people in the West, still known for transience, could build community and connection on their dramatic piece of ground. His advice was simple, something the Indians learned long ago: "Find your place. Dig in. And defend it."

Anyone who cares about the fate of the West must be open to new voices, and authentic ones at that. That often means being alive to contradiction. Think of this collection as a cabin full of storytellers, ambiguous in the whole. But cozy, as well.

Preface

Who Are the Writers on the Range?

Thirty years ago, a quiet-spoken Wyoming rancher started a funky little newspaper about the vast American West. His name was Tom Bell, and the paper was called *High Country News*.

Though he loved the West's natural wonders, Bell wasn't interested in just telling readers about the best fishing streams, the most beautiful forests, or the places with great powder skiing. He had darker news to impart: The hand of humanity was reaching out to defile the once seemingly untouchable interior West. Unless the people spoke out, Bell thought that everything he loved about the region—from clean air and water to abundant wildlife and the magnificent land itself—would be lost.

During the paper's first years, Bell took on a number of the West's sacred cows: He hammered on his fellow ranchers for indiscriminately poisoning and shooting eagles and other predators; he railed against the giant energy companies (and the politicians who were in their pockets) and their plans to strip-mine the high plains for coal; he tackled the U.S. Forest Service for allowing timber companies to clear-cut the national forests.

The pages were filled with the voices of westerners—ranchers, environmentalists, miners, loggers, politicians, hunters—all arguing over their very own future.

This passionate cacophony can still be found every other week in the pages of *High Country News*, and it is the reason why, three years ago, the paper started "Writers on the Range," its syndicated columns project.

Turn to the opinion pages of many newspapers in the West and you'll find what's in most any newspaper in America: a large serving of mostly conservative syndicated national columnists commenting on a small plate of hot-button national issues and a smattering of local columnists writing about the latest local brouhaha. What's missing are distinctly regional voices jousting on the many issues that every western community faces today, whether they be the titanic battles over public-land management or the social, political, and economic fallout of rapid growth.

We know these voices exist, because we have listened to and projected them for thirty years. Yet until we started Writers on the Range, the depth of this region's writing talent was hardly imaginable. Every week, we distribute three Writers on the Range essays to newspapers throughout the West—one hundred fifty-six a year. And the well has never come close to running dry.

Living in the Runaway West features the best of Writers on the Range. You may recognize some of the writers, especially those who are well-established authors, veteran journalists, and political heavies. Other contributors are newer to the world of words, and they come from many walks of life. In this book you will hear from a couple of ranchers, a city councilman, a county commissioner, several environmental activists, a state wildlife biologist, and a river guide, to name a few.

Though the essays are short and to the point, they paint a big, broad picture of the West at the beginning of a new millennium. Parts of the image are beautiful. Much of it is not. All of it is sharply focused.

So sit back and listen to the Writers on the Range as they tell their stories of angry sagebrush rebels, brooding environmentalists, vanishing wolves and bears, beleaguered cows, bloodied hunters, sanguine slot-machine junkies, clueless monster-home owners, underpaid immigrant hotel workers, corrupt politicians, and smooth-talking developers.

If they make you cry, laugh, or rage, so much the better. Tom Bell, who still lives in his beloved town of Lander, Wyoming, will be proud that the great western dialogue he started thirty years ago is alive and kicking.

—*Paul Larmer*

For more information about Writers on the Range or High Country News, *write to HCN, P.O. Box 1090, Paonia, CO 81428; 970-527-4898. Visit HCN's website at www.hcn.org.*

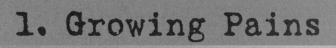

1. Growing Pains

Why I'm Against It All
—*Ken Wright*

For two years I wrote an environmental column for a small western-Colorado newspaper.

It wasn't hard work, really. I just rambled on for 600 words each week about the rugged landscape around us and then offered some helpful observations and suggestions: that housing developments really aren't good elk habitat, that the local ski area is big enough already, that the Forest Service shouldn't execute one of the area's last old-growth ponderosa stands, that the Bureau of Reclamation shouldn't insert yet another concrete suppository in yet another nearby river, and so on.

Believe it or not, some of those columns drew complaints.

Most of the complaints began with the same general introduction: "Hey you (insert your favorite adjective here), you weren't born here, were you?"

I appreciated the time folks took to offer me feedback in those notes (sometimes with painstakingly cut-out and taped-on letters) and phone calls (often after midnight, when the rates are low). It connected me to the many other labeled "newcomers" who have migrated to the West and dared to point out the waste, stupidity, and greed dismantling this fantastic place.

Still, I'm not afraid to admit I wasn't born a westerner. And I am not afraid to admit—as even many "environmentalists" are for fear of weakening their credibility—that I am against most of the changes happening here: bigger airports, new roads, the widening and straightening and grading of old roads, Wal-Marts, Kmarts, Qwik Marts, corporate resorts, ski-area expansions, water developments, golf courses, casinos, marinas, campgrounds, trailhead parking, brochures, maps, promotional websites, and about anything any chamber of commerce anywhere does. And on and on.

I say, stop it all: Keep the roads a mess, the infrastructure archaic, the water scarce, and the transportation hell. Don't let the profiteers gouge out the amenities and infrastructure luring the urban refugees now ravaging the West, and they won't come.

With every incremental "improvement" in the West, there are a dozen people for whom that improvement makes it just easy enough to live here.

And once they get settled, they know it would be perfect if their new town only had a (you name it). And that new improvement just makes it comfortable enough for the next dozen, who just wish their new town (you name it again).

I'm not saying we should shut the door. Anyone can live here if they want, as long as they're willing to do it on this place's terms. If folks don't want to give up nice roads, easy access to air transport, bluegrass lawns, tee times, specialty coffee shops, shopping malls, and on-ramps to the information superhighway, then there's most of the rest of the country already paved over, roaded through, and wired up for them.

I know. I used to live there.

Like many native westerners, there's a class of us newcomers who love small working towns and wild country. Call us rural refugees. We're from different states, but we're from the same state of mind—we worship the precious backcountry and close-knit communities that still survive in the West, and we settled here willing to sacrifice urban conveniences, high-tech luxuries, and fat paychecks to have those things. We would've been happy to stay wherever we're from, but we saw our native rural towns and landscapes crushed by the glassy-eyed cult of economics that chants "Growth Is Good" and whose vision extends only to the end of the next fiscal year.

And so I say to the longtime lovers of the West who resent all *newcomers*, if you listen to us we can offer valuable, hard-earned lessons that you'll never hear from a politician, real-estate developer, chain-store corporation, or mega-resort.

We learned the hard way that you can't have it both ways. We know that the planning, studying, sloganeering ("Smart Growth" is Colorado's favorite platitude), mitigation, and grumblings about the free market and private property only soothe your conscience and cut loose the profiteers; they do nothing to stop the strip mining of the culture and countryside that is the inevitable cost of growth.

That is why we can't keep quiet when we hear again the familiar optimistic and hypnotic hymns: Growth is good. We can control growth. We'll all get rich. Just a little more improvement. There's another valley over the ridge, and another river over the hill.

And that is why I'm against it all.

My Beautiful Ranchette

—Susan Ewing

My name is Susan. I live on a ranchette.

In the growth-pained, environmentally conscious West, this is as serious a confession as alcoholism or cruelty to animals. Some argue it is cruelty to animals, in the form of competition with wildlife for habitat. In today's local newspaper, I could pick out my place in the huge, front-page, aerial, color photo under the black headline, "Tracking Sprawl." This isn't the first time my neighbors and I have seen our homes on a front page illustrating all that is "ugly" about growth in our south-central Montana community. Last spring we made the cover of the Greater Yellowstone Coalition newsletter. I studied the picture while walking back to my house from the mailbox; as a member of that environmental organization, I read the newsletter with interest.

Yes, living in town would be more environmentally correct than living on a twenty-acre parcel. I don't like sprawl either, don't like it here in the foothills any more than I like the filling in of irreplaceable agricultural land within the newly expanded limits of my burgeoning little city. But I have had to swallow my resentment of all the construction, because there's nothing worse than the "last-one-in-slam-the-door" syndrome.

I respect and admire people who live in high-density housing situations because of environmental convictions. But my need for quiet, space, the company of wildlife, and the chance to settle directly into the ecosystem (of which I am a part) is stronger than my sense of obligation to an urban density solution. I love my place, love it with a physical feeling that expands inside me like a summer cloud. Acknowledging that we disrupted wildlife patterns by building our house here, we have tried to amend our presence: Our dogs are contained in a fenced yard; we conserve water and participate in water-use studies; we limit trips to town; we don't have a cat. I pull Canada thistles until my hands are too sore to grip a pencil, and weeds that won't pull, I spray carefully with the most benign herbicide I can find. Over the years, native shrubs, grasses, and wildflowers have reclaimed roots previously grazed down by the cattle that used to run on this ground.

I know where mushrooms grow and where flickers nest. I feel whole and hopeful and incredibly blessed watching mule deer rest near the house or catching sight of the resident ermine running by with a vole in its mouth. Mountain cottontails lounge under the car and chickadees are a constant, cheerful influence.

I'm happy to compromise and work for responsible occupancy of this beautiful land. That's one reason I support organizations such as the Greater Yellowstone Coalition. I am in favor of planned and managed growth: The concept of clustering houses when geographically feasible to leave more open space is good, and I strongly endorse much stricter covenants regarding water use and the control of pets, weeds, and erosion.

Unmitigated sprawl stresses wildlife, land resources, and emotions and is a serious concern everywhere in the United States, not just in the West. It's simply easier to see here, and perhaps more painfully felt since we are still trying to hold onto something special: neighborliness, clean air, safe streets, easy access to hunting and fishing and hiking.

Other people lived in these foothills before I did; our neighbors have found their arrowheads. I want to live here, too. It's sad that there are now so many of us that we are being advised to remove ourselves from the land-scape in order to protect it. This breaks my heart.

In the final analysis, sprawl is only the deeply troubling symptom of a much larger problem: too many people. Planned and managed growth needs to be applied to human populations, too. According to the United States Census Bureau, more than six billion people live on our planet, near-ly three hundred million of them in the United States. The number of people in the United States is projected to double by the year 2050. Where will all those bodies live? Will they stay put in overcrowded cities? In only about a dozen years, traffic is predicted to increase over 400 per-cent on freeways and 100 percent on local roads. Less than half of our nation's original wetlands remain, and only 1 percent of tall-grass prairie and 15 percent of old-growth forests.

No doubt ranchettes figure in there somewhere, but at what level of blame? I wonder if I can trade the 2.5 children I didn't have, plus an annual contribution to Planned Parenthood, for the promise that the next headline illustration of ugly sprawl will leave my beautiful ranchette out of it.

Hanging On in Montana
—*Ray Ring*

On June 2, it was a bit nippy here in Bozeman, Montana. I walked around town wearing a sweater over a long-sleeved shirt. The wind came up and the sky churned with gray and black clouds. Foolishly, I'd left the house without an insulated jacket.

The wind sharpened in the evening, as I watered the trees in my yard, and my hands went numb. The next morning, June 3, the storm front arrived, slapping surly wet snowflakes down on everything.

It's been four years since my family and I uprooted from metro Tucson and moved seriously north to here. Old friends we left behind still ask me versions of "What the heck is it with Montana?"

There's a mystique, exaggerated good and bad, to Montana these days. To most people, it is halfway off the planet, a series of pretty but unreal scenes from *The Horse Whisperer* mixed with jokes about the militia/Unabomber fringe and no daytime speed limit, wahoo!

It doesn't have much to do with the day-to-day real thing.

The Horse Whisperer was filmed around here, but it didn't show this: We live in a county with Montana's most popular ski resort, Montana's biggest university, more than sixty small high-tech companies that have chosen to locate here, two engineering firms that specialize in rebuilding trout streams, and the fiercest competition in latte and gourmet bakeries. Twenty-acre parcels of nothing but grass close to town are up to $300,000 or more now, ranches carved into ranchette development.

Yet it's true I once saw a woman pull up in front of the downtown library on an actual horse. The lead news photo in today's paper shows real-life local cowboys herding cattle from winter to summer range. Truckloads of baled hay rumble down main streets. The Old West is still alive here, barely, even as the New West money flows in.

The money swirls around a minority: the second-home buyers and modem commuters. The rest of Montana is still mostly agricultural, and even those of us not directly selling wheat and cattle for below cost are not well off. The state ranks roughly last in average salaries; our governor is the lowest paid, our university profs about the lowest paid.

We're here because we want to be, but it's hard to make it here, and you can see that in the lack of people. As 80 to 90 percent of modern westerners crowd into the region's exploding cities, Montana has nothing on the scale of Denver, no Salt Lake City or Phoenix, not even a Tucson or a Boise or a Spokane. Instead we have modest islands of settlement floating on a vast sea of ranches, mountains, and weather rolling to the horizon.

Dealing with bad weather, isolation, and tight money, Montanans tend to respect each other for hanging on. The whole state has the neighborly feel of a small town. We have our share of mindless violence, but there is statistical evidence of less tension than in crowded places. Our county has 60,000 people but, on average, less than one murder per year. Figured per capita, the local murder rate is one-seventh, maybe just one-tenth, of what it is in the urban West.

We don't worry much when our kids roam around town on their own. A lot of houses and cars here never get locked. To cash a local check, usually it isn't necessary to show an ID.

Our most powerful official, the governor, is listed in the phone book—his home number. We can call him up nights or weekends and complain about taxes or whatever. He's a Republican, at least pretending to be moderate, who wears cowboy boots. At important social-political gatherings he drinks beer out of the bottle.

When the governor came to my daughter's elementary school to speak to a student assembly, he drove himself in a modest sedan, no highfalutin limo and chauffeur, no staff entourage, no bodyguards. The governor did use the official helicopter recently to drop into a country K-8 school, where he spoke to the graduating class of one.

Everyone here seems closer to the land—even the car dealers. The local Ford dealer bases his entire TV ad campaign on pictures of himself fishing this or that river. A car dealer in Butte runs statewide TV ads in which he rides a large, shaggy, horned buffalo through his car lot as he urges customers to come on down.

Even the generic public-service TV ads are natural. My favorite runs all winter. It shows shot after shot of blizzards pounding the roads and some poor drivers under siege, climaxing with a line of narration: "Montana's snowplow drivers—where would we be without them?"

Clearly we're in this Montana thing together. In the history of keeping weather records in Bozeman, there is no day of the year on which snow has never fallen. Meanwhile, as people move around the West looking to realize some dream, most pay for their *Horse Whisperer* ticket but decide not to move here because of the bad weather and the tough, humbling economy. We enjoy the most effective forms of growth control.

Cracking the Contractor's Code
—*Marty Jones*

They call it the "dream of home ownership," but for my wife and me, buying our first house in Colorado was more of a nightmare. Thanks to a long list of pseudo contractors and wannabe builders, our home purchase was a grueling saga of delays, shabby work, and tears. Instead of the happy moment we saw in real-estate commercials, crossing the threshold in our first home was a dark event filled with dread and questions.

Had the hot air balloon that symbolizes our agent's company actually floated in for our big moment, it would have surely crashed and burned on our roof, its pilot without experience, a license, insurance, or a clue.

Such is the plight of the house hunter in the rapidly expanding New West, where the folks doing the building enjoy a builder's market. Because of this boom and the resultant shortage of reputable craftspeople, consumers are left to deal with an unsavory lot of fly-by-nights. Doing so means signing pacts with a new breed of outlaw guns-for-hire, whose language rivals that of White House aides when it comes to avoiding accountability. To help you skip the loss of dollars, time, weight, and hair that my wife and I endured in having our homestead completed, here's a quick primer on the secret language of the Front Range fix-it person.

For example, in the jargon of the Colorado Contractor's Code, "references" does not mean satisfied clients. It means family members who pose as clients and offer glowing testimonials about make-believe work. When asking for references, be sure and ask that your potential contractors exclude next of kin and include at least one person for whom they have actually performed work.

Should your contractors ever proclaim "This is how I normally do it," beware. This means they've never done it before and that their work will resemble what you'd expect from a sign painter/cab driver/cook posing as a professional builder. If the real-estate agents for that same faux foreman vouch for any aspect of their client's work, plan on redoing it once you move in. Based on the tile and grout that continue to break loose of our floor, our refurbishing expert "normally" places mosaic tile directly over warped, dirty, hundred-year-old wooden flooring.

This same skilled craftsman installed a novel kitchen cabinet that faces directly into the side of our stove. We call this permanently sealed crypt of a cupboard the "Llewellyn cabinet," in honor of its esteemed inventor. The man we consulted with to fix this kitchen accessory enlightened us on the secret meaning of "character." After talking a blue streak about his over the phone, he disappeared for three weeks before arriving to offer an estimate. His price would have bought a room in our house, but he had an explanation for the lofty bill: "This is too small a job for me. I really don't want to do it."

"First thing in the morning" is another phrase to fear. If you hear this after signing a contract for work in your home, it typically means the person you've just hired will use your materials deposit to buy controlled substances and pay his bondsman. Likewise, it could mean "I have your money and I'm using it to pay for the materials on the other houses I'm trashing." Or it could also be decoded as "I'll see you in several weeks, during which I won't return your calls."

There are other terms to be aware of as well. If the person you've enlisted to fix your furnace (say, the fourth person you've hired to do so) finishes up the job with "That oughta work for you," you've got trouble. This seemingly friendly comment means "I have no idea how to fix this, but I want to get out of here before you realize it." Likewise, if your electrician claims he's "the best in town," he's really the worst. After he incorrectly wires your lights and disappears with your check, all the electricians after him will carefully critique his shoddy work while boasting of their own kingly qualifications.

If your builder mentions giving you "your money's worth," change the locks on your doors immediately. Standing before freshly painted trim replete with drips and sags, our painter explained his value-added impressionistic work with "Look, it's not like this is some $250,000 home in Highlands Ranch." No, it's a row house for half that—pick up your six-pack and get out.

Of course, not every builder on the high plains is unaccountable, unskilled, and underhanded. We've actually heard stories, albeit unconfirmed, of contractors doing what they promise, on time and under budget. In fact, we think we've just lined up one such savior to finish our basement. He even spent a couple hours surveying the room while addressing our fears and detailing the quality of his work. Better yet, he promised to call us in a couple of days with a price quote.

That was six weeks ago.

The ABCs for Developers
—Norm Wallen

Anyone living in a growing western community understands how development can change the character of the place where they live. Yet most of us are uninformed about the development process itself. We curse the powers that be when new subdivisions and strip malls go up or we get stuck in traffic jams that didn't exist last year, but we don't really understand the rules, both hidden and apparent, that created this new reality.

I was ignorant, too, until I was elected to the Flagstaff, Arizona, city council three years ago. Since then, I've learned more about the dealings between developers, government officials, and citizens than I really wanted to know. I've been accused of hating developers (not yet entirely true), so I'd like to make amends. Here's some advice for them, free of charge.

1. *Keep your deals secret as long as possible.* Never let the public in on your arrangements with landowners or your intentions for a piece of property until you have to. Typically, you will first have informal conversations with the staff of whichever government unit has to give approval; these are easy to keep quiet. At some point, you will have to make formal application, leading up to formal staff review at a public meeting. It's pretty easy to keep the public ignorant of this, as well, unless there is a really nosy reporter in town. This is all you have to do if your plan does not require a rezoning, no matter how offensive your development may be. People still ask me how the Flagstaff city council could allow an ugly fortress hotel at the major entrance to the city. The truth is, we never saw the plans because the developer followed this first principle so well.

2. *Do your best to muscle staff.* Remember, county and city planning staff are obligated to help you comply with those onerous ordinances—usually engineering, public safety, resource protection, and, God forbid, design standards. Since ordinances are legal documents, there is always some wiggle room. And since you, the beleaguered developer, have to pay for analysis of impacts on traffic, water, sewer, and the rest, subject only to review by staff, you have a big head start. In a recent case in my town, it was the neighbors—not the staff—who caught the developer when his assessment

of existing tree canopy was "slightly off"—by about 125 percent. Be sure your team (architect, engineer, lawyer) pushes the limits. Staff planners are generally overworked and susceptible to being worn down.

3. *Bully public officials with the stick.* If you must get an up-zoning to higher density—to put 1,000 homes on a parcel zoned for 70, for example—you will have to face the Planning and Zoning Commission, a body made up of appointed citizens who make recommendations to the elected officials. They will, of course, differ in their degree of worship of the Development Trinity: Profit—the father, Private Property Rights—the son, and Growth—the unholy ghost. But use these deeply held beliefs to your advantage: Argue that you are entitled to the up-zoning if your plan meets the requirements of the new zone (even though you are not; most ordinances require any rezoning to be in the interest of the community). Make noises that anything but approval will force you to sue the town for an illegal "taking"of your property. And if the public is likely to give you trouble at a public hearing, outgun them with a carefully rehearsed presentation (lots of pictures) augmented by testimonials on your good intentions, even from those who stand to profit from your project.

4. *Placate them with the carrot.* If you can't convince staff or citizens that their concerns about your project are baseless, argue that they can be fixed with "mitigation" measures. This tactic is becoming more difficult to pull off, since the public is now more aware of floodplains flooding, hillsides falling down, unbearable traffic congestion, and unfinished landscaping (promised by previous developers). Still, belief in the technical fix is so strong that you will likely prevail.

One way to sell your project is to claim that it has an affordable housing component. If you can stomach it (some can), argue that affordable means affordable to all income levels; never agree that it means a home within the capability of a family in the bottom 40 percent of average income. You might even use cost as an excuse to end run the review process and try to obtain approval directly from the governing body.

5. *Finally, remember that your well-paid lawyer can challenge your development agreement with the government should you decide the requirements are just too much of a hassle to meet.* City fathers are loathe to blow the whistle on a development once it's underway.

I realize that most of you developers already know all this. But we do want a level playing field, now, don't we?

You Are Where You Eat

—*Mary Sojourner*

Fifteen years ago my Cockney friend Ashley, a guy so thoroughly in love with the American West that his mum persuaded him as a kid to eat liver by claiming it was buffalo, said, "Let's go to the Grand Canyon. You'll love it."

We lived in the heart of a wannabe-Manhattan eastern city. I'd been part of a successful late-sixties movement to revitalize the dying town and, as far as I was concerned, Out West was desert, which meant hot, brown, and ugly. Plus no barbecue, no jazz, no decent coffee.

"Thanks, but no thanks," I said. "The Grand Canyon's a tourist trap, nothing but hamburger stands, souvenir shops, and too many people."

He bet me fifty bucks it wasn't. I said I'd go if we could stop at Hopi, which I believed to be a mysterious utopia set high in gorgeous mysterious cliffs—and if we ate at the local diners, barbecue pits, and mom-and-pop restaurants in Jane and Michael Sterns's book *Road Food*. The Sterns's criteria were simple: the place had to be within ten miles of an interstate and the food within range of heaven.

He agreed. We took off, and on an interstate in Indiana, despite truly compelling barbecue and the best homemade biscuits I'd ever lavished with country butter, I looked around at miles of malls and announced that I hated the West and wanted to go home. "I've got fifty bucks riding on this," he said, "and Indianapolis isn't the West." I whined a little more, then flipped through *Road Food* to find the next great breakfast stop.

The Canyon wasn't Sceneryland, the Hopi dancers moved not across a ledge, but in a dusty plaza, rattles and bells and song lulling the urban beat of my heart into rare calm, and too soon I cried most of the unbearable drive east—toward what was no longer home.

Two years later, I moved to Flagstaff, Arizona, lured by the long, sweet volcanic line of the San Francisco Peaks, the scent of Ponderosa pine, the proximity of fierce blue desert shadows, the fact that most of the women seemed to live in faded flannel shirts and Levis, and Macy's Coffee Shops' cinnamon bear-claw pastries, El Charro's chicken-fried steak slathered with two different chilis, Mountainaire Tavern's mega-omelets and real home fries that would sustain a normal person for a week.

I believed I had found a place so true, so down-home, so genuine, that time had passed it by and would, forever.

I was wrong. Our town's charm was lost on too few. Subdivision by subdivision, second home by second home, designer cowgirl outfit by outfit, we grew.

At 50,000 people, the chains came in. Motel 6 and Hampton Inn Suites and thirty other identi-kit motels slid into the outskirts of town. Fazoli's and IHOP and Olive Garden drove out wildflowers, prairie dogs, and the possibility of real food. Tourists on their way to the Grand Canyon or Sedona could sleep and eat in perfect tedium, confident that where they rested and what they ate were identical to everything back home. You could now haul Dayton or Syracuse with you, much as you might a monster fifth-wheel trailer complete with computerized blinds, satellite dish, and the acrylic Ohio-green lawn you roll out on campground asphalt.

Our town lost too many local restaurants. More are hovering on the brink of fiscal belly flop—as are trading posts and bookstores; clothing shops and yogurt stands; bead, furniture, and hardware stores. Downtown's okay, thanks to a hard-hitting, savvy local merchants' organization. The peripheries are alive and well as tourists pull numbly off Interstate 40 and go for what they are media-barraged to think they want. In the middle ground, on the east side, south side, in places that are neither chic nor cliché, owners struggle to keep what's genuine and unique alive.

Every dollar spent in a franchise moves a local business closer to death, moves Flagstaff closer to being Atlanta or Salt Lake City or Los Angeles or wherever the touring hordes are fleeing. Unless those of us who live here support local business—and the people who visit take the fifteen minutes it requires to drive our streets, ask a local's advice, or read through the local paper—corpoburger quick-stops and Pacific Rim microwaved spaghetti dealers will drive out the tiny taco shack on the side street off Old Route 66, the coffeehouse where they roast coffee so carefully it makes Seattle's finest taste like brewed sawdust, and the family-run Thai spot whose lunch specials cost less than a BLT at Denny's and remind you that heat and delicacy can exist on the same plate.

All western towns will look and taste the same. A taco in Cleveland will be the clone of a taco in Tucumcari, in Moab, in Redding. The family pulling off Interstate 40 somewhere west of Gallup will pull into an exact copy of the outskirts of their own town. They will wonder why they came all that way, and the next year, they will stay home.

Single in the West
—*Michelle Nijhuis*

I moved from Tucson to a small town in western Colorado just in time for my twenty-fourth birthday last winter. At first, I couldn't believe how lucky I was to have stumbled across this place. The mountains in my backyard, the fresh fruit in the summer, the skiing in the winter, and the weekend potlucks with friends: It couldn't be better, I told my envious, traffic-weary friends in Portland and San Francisco. I had a dream job in paradise.

My friends and neighbors knew better. I first got an inkling that my life in the rural West might not be perfect when the owner of our local co-op, a perfectly sweet woman, started asking me if I'd met any nice boys lately. Later, when an apparently eligible man about my age moved to town, the cashier at the deli asked me how we were getting along. Soon, I couldn't deny to my out-of-town friends that I was going alone to square dances on Saturday nights. They stopped sounding envious and started saying things like "It's a little bit isolated there, isn't it?"

Somehow, over the past year, I've acquired an identity I never expected to have. In a town full of couples, I've become a Young Single Person—and I'm wearing my label like a bad haircut. Everyone wants to help me out. My boss leaves the *Western Singles Network* newspaper on my desk, and advertisements for singles supper clubs and mixers in nearby towns inevitably head my way. Neighbors extend innocent-sounding dinner invitations, then introduce me to their second cousin Bob from Florida, who just happened to drop by for a visit on that very same evening.

When friends hear that I work with four other single people under thirty, they all have the same reaction. "Well?" they ask, raising their eyebrows suggestively. "What do you mean you haven't met any nice boys lately?" I shake my head and remind them that office romance is a dangerous game in this post-Monica world, but they shamelessly plow ahead, ever eager to find me a date. Last week, a friend actually ended a session of not-so-gentle prodding by saying "I mean, who else *is* there?"

It's starting to get to me. I'm doing things I never would have done when I was happily unattached and hanging out in hip Portland coffee shops.

When I do venture out of town, I realize that I've lost any ability to be cool and aloof ("Stop staring at him," an embarrassed friend whispered to me last fall at a Bay Area bar). On slow Friday nights, my eyes linger on the singles' websites advertised in the back pages of *Harper's*. I catch myself composing personals ads in my head: "Twenty-something female journalist looking for irreverent, bookish fellow willing to relocate." No, I think, grasping for my lost pride, it would never work—we'd always have to explain how we met.

I even daydream about old college buddies: So what if he lives in New Jersey and gives money to the Newt Gingrich Commemorative Library Fund? Maybe we have more in common than I used to think. Actually, forget it—this month, he and his new wife are listed in the "Unions" section of my college alumni magazine. Speaking of unions, wedding invitations keep showing up in the mail, and I'm collecting a disturbing number of bridesmaids' dresses. Should I be worried?

It's no joke that the rural West can be a lonely place for anyone, of any age. You can find solitude, silence, and peace here, but all of us mistake those things for loneliness once in a while, and it sometimes takes a spectacular camping trip or a night of skiing under the stars to remind us why we choose to live where we do. My neighbors know this, too, and I can't blame them for wanting to make my life a little easier—even if their help sometimes has the opposite effect.

Fortunately, there have been more than enough incredible sunsets here to keep me from wanting to trade places with my city friends. Sometimes, late at night, my friends even admit to me that their calendars aren't as full as they'd like me to think. In the city, everyone *expects* them to have dates stacked three deep, and they always feel like they're coming up short.

So being single is tough no matter where you are, and I guess I'm lucky to be toughing it out in such a beautiful place. But if you happen to be an irreverent, bookish fellow willing to relocate . . . oh, never mind. I'm going skiing.

Wyoming: The Last Tough Place
—Tom Reed

There's a Wyoming hunter I know who lucked out one year, in more ways than one.

He's a mule man. I've never seen him ride anything else. This particular year he drew a coveted bighorn sheep license, an opportunity that comes along perhaps once in a lifetime. You have to be devoted to be a bighorn sheep hunter. He was. He scouted his area, got in shape, and prepared for months. When the hunt finally arrived, he was on a mule in the wild country.

One evening, after a long day, his mule "unloaded" him and he found himself on the ground getting stomped. He rolled out from beneath the mule's hooves, clambered back to his feet, and got aboard, then rode to camp. Later that night he awoke unable to breathe, thinking he was going to die. So he took a long ride on a mule and then in a helicopter to a hospital.

The doctors found a punctured lung, busted ribs, and a broken collarbone. They told him he was out of commission and could kiss the sheep license good-bye. At any age, let alone sixty-something, he was lucky to be alive.

What the doctors didn't realize was that this was one tough son of a gun. A month later, he was back on the mountain with his mules, looking to bag his sheep.

I think about this Wyoming mule man whenever I hear about Wyoming's grim economic picture and hear people complaining about the lack of services and jobs in this emptiest, loneliest place in the country. Most Rocky Mountain states have boomed in recent years, buoyed by an influx of jobs and newcomers. Wyoming hasn't. If the economic horizon of the New West is a gentle hill of flowers, bathed in sunlight, then Wyoming's is a steep, windswept, rocky ridge where little more than sagebrush grows. There are still fewer people here—just 480,000—than in any other state in the nation.

Wyoming has a shortage of everything from physicians to shopping malls. Big airlines shun the state because there are so few customers. Wyoming ranks dead last—fiftieth among the states—in employment growth. Wages haven't even kept up with inflation and are well below the national average.

To stay here, you have to be something of a throwback to the Great Depression, a jack-of-all-trades willing to try different things. I have a friend whose resumé includes wilderness ranger, outdoor educator, cabinetmaker, finish carpenter, backhoe operator, horse logger, plumber, contractor, farmer, sugar beet truck driver, and small-scale rancher. He could move with his young family somewhere else, make more, and do less, but he doesn't want to. He likes Wyoming, so he does more for less.

Here, you can be served a beer at the local watering hole by a state senator between legislative sessions. The man who hammers shoes on your horses' hooves might also double as the bank president. You can still pass a personal check in a town on the other side of the state (often without even showing identification) or stop to help a stranded motorist.

Former Wyoming Governor Mike Sullivan called Wyoming a small town with extremely long streets. That's an accurate portrayal, I think. I've been amazed to find people who know people I know even though I'm 300 miles away from home.

I get frustrated sometimes by the staunch conservatives in this state who hate wolves yet love industrial development. At the same time, I value them as part of this rugged, lonely place. I stood toe-to-toe with two men late one night, arguing the virtues of predators, from coyotes to grizzlies. The next morning, we were still friends. We just had different opinions.

There are those who would change Wyoming, make it grow and support a large population. They claim that Wyoming lacks culture and sophistication. Wyoming does have a culture, though it doesn't include coffeehouses and symphonies. It's a culture of individualism, sparsely, but vividly, populated with tough people like that mule man.

I like the fact that there are no decent commercial airports and damn few trendy malls here. I like that you can walk or ride into the high country or desert for days without seeing anyone else. I like knowing that in those places, man isn't the toughest creature in the woods—the grizzly fills that role.

It shouldn't be easy to live in Wyoming. If it was, anybody could do it.

Crazy Horse Must Be Laughing
—*Dave Gowdey*

This year, for the first time since Arizona was settled, hunting will not be allowed in the Walnut Canyon area around Flagstaff. The wealthy new inhabitants of the area, from southern California mostly, don't favor hunting. At the same time, Flagstaff has now seen its second Arizona Opera Company production of Richard Wagner's *Ring* series. The main street of town was temporarily renamed Valkyrie Street in honor of this event.

To borrow a line from Bob Dylan, "The times they are a changin'."

One hundred and fifty years ago my relatives invaded the West, dispossessed the local inhabitants, and ran roughshod over their culture. Proud peoples with centuries of tradition were burned off their land, herded into rural ghettos, and reduced to beggary. In a less violent, but no less sure, manner the same thing is happening again. Perhaps there is Karma.

In fact, it's happening in other parts of the world as well. In Scotland, the locals call them "White Settlers"—affluent urbanites from London who are buying up many of the beautiful areas of rural Scotland, putting up summer cottages, and fencing them off from the locals. As market forces push rural property prices up, the local inhabitants are having trouble paying their ever-increasing property taxes. Being Scots, they have reacted in a rather direct manner to this modern English invasion. The year I finished my graduate studies in Aberdeen, twenty-six summer homes were burned to the ground.

Here in the western United States, the process is called "Aspenization" after the economic slaughter of the innocents that happened in Aspen in the late 1970s and early 1980s. Wealthy outsiders, mostly from southern California, fell in love with the small mining-turned-skiing town and began buying up all the property. They pushed property prices so high that lawyers and doctors making almost $100,000 per year now receive government assistance so they can afford housing in Aspen. Locals, working for tourist-economy wages, no longer have any hope of being able to afford housing in town. They commute from rural ghettos to clean the toilets and mow the lawns of the rich and famous. A few realtors got fabulously wealthy, but as usual the majority of the townsfolk got screwed.

As southern Californians continue to flee the urban monstrosity they have created, and refugees stream from Chicago and Detroit, this cultural destruction of the West proceeds at an ever-increasing pace. Jackson Hole, Bozeman, Taos, Flagstaff, Boulder, Ketchum, Prescott, Telluride, Moab, Santa Fe—the list of towns that have been Aspenized or are facing Aspenization continues to grow.

Urbanites who read this list may chuckle to themselves. One person's Aspenization is another's civilization. The fact is that what is going on is another campaign of cultural genocide against the rural West. The Rape of the West, Part II.

Although we are both Americans, I have as much in common with a resident of Los Angeles or Orange County or Chicago as I do with a Frenchman. The ethics and values of these urban refugees baffle me. I cannot understand why they build a golf course in the middle of beautiful mountain meadows so they can build expensive houses on the fairways. I cannot understand why they increasingly demand that public schools teach their children morality, while they oppose increased funding for education. I cannot understand their instinctive belief that the poor should be punished for lacking the moral fiber to rise above poverty.

I am puzzled why they remain unconcerned when their policemen shoot and harass poor blacks and Hispanics but are outraged that we shoot coyotes. I am dumbfounded that they bring their hoodlum children to our school system, hoping that our rural values will change them, yet they threaten to sue the teacher that disciplines little Jimmy.

Finally, I cannot fathom why they move to an idyllic small town and then demand that more concrete and asphalt be poured over the countryside to provide the amenities they enjoyed in Los Angeles.

Unless the citizens of the rural West decide to prohibit the construction of housing targeted at affluent immigrants, this wave of urban refugees will continue to spill over the region like sewage from a backed-up toilet. These newcomers will continue to abolish hunting, and rodeos, and god knows what else, and replace them with fat ladies singing the "Luftwaffe Serenade" by that anti-Semitic bastard Wagner.

I sometimes wonder if some Sioux, and Cheyenne, and Navajo, and Apache braves weren't saying these same things around a campfire a century ago. I bet they were. Crazy Horse must be laughing himself silly.

A Newcomer's Old Story
—Paul Larmer

"I'm a third-generation Coloradoan," the man tells me, leaning in close across the kitchen table inside his self-built home. "My people settled country down in southern Colorado."

I read between the lines: "I belong here. Do you?"

I know the answer. I am a newcomer—only five years in western Colorado. I own a house, but I hold no title to this landscape.

I could tell him that I am a fifth-generation Californian, born in the state that my great-great grandfather unluckily settled in the year after the 1849 gold rush. But people here don't think much of Californians. We are the latest invaders—and the cause of unaffordable housing and trendy coffeehouses.

I just nod.

My companion then surprises me. "You know my wife and I are still considered outsiders, and we've lived here twenty-one years," he says. "Unless your kids marry into one of the old area families, you'll always be an outsider."

That's what fascinates me about the West: It's old and new at the same time, and there are as many shades of nativeness as there are varieties of broken-down trucks in its weedy backyards.

I remember when rural western counties began passing ordinances proclaiming that livestock grazing, logging, and mining were their "custom and culture" and should be preserved no matter how destructive or uneconomic they might be. These counties were saying "The West is mine because I got here first."

"First" is a relative term. I loved the editorial a few years ago by a Native American writer from Wyoming questioning the custom-and-culture crowd's sense of time. Why, Debra Thunder asked, should society declare the recent activities of newcomers from Europe the law of the land, while ignoring the customs and cultures of Native peoples, who have lived on the land for hundreds of generations?

The truth is that the West has always been a place in motion, culturally and biologically. Before the mountain men were evicted by settlers, Native tribes vied for turf and resources, pushing each other in and out of various valleys and canyons just as surely as real-estate developers and the people they serve now push around the "old-timers."

The only difference—and it's important—is the scale and speed of change. Within just one century people from every nook of the United States and from around the world have reshaped the West, blocking and rerouting rivers, turning desert into lush agricultural fields, and, most recently, building sprawling suburbs.

Yet we newcomers still come, drawn to a region that appears wild and untouched next to the tamed habitats of the East. But it's not untouched. The plant and animal world is experiencing the same kind of change as the human world. In fact, the two are inexorably linked.

Tamarisk, an Asian shrub that escaped the gardens of southern California, chokes thousands of miles in the Colorado River drainage, pushing out native cottonwoods and willows. Spotted knapweed, cheatgrass, leafy spurge, and a host of other annual grasses and flowering exotics cover millions of acres of former grasslands. European starlings and finches dominate my bird feeder, which hangs from a Chinese elm.

I should feel at home among such exotic company, yet part of me wants to join the loggers and ranchers to fight exotic plants and animals and even human newcomers like myself. How can the West accommodate so many newcomers without losing its identity?

As a child, my family moved every three or four years on the trail of my father's corporate career. We were American weeds, and we lodged temporarily in Los Angeles, Chicago, St. Louis, and Philadelphia. Yet these were never home. Family, not place, defined my home, which is why I still search for my homeland.

I often take my children to the cemetery on the mesa above my new town. We look out over the valley and wander among the graves, reading the names of the families who toiled to become natives of this place. I recognize a few of the family names, but most of them are gone. I wonder if my children will stay here or whether they, like most of the kids around here, will drift elsewhere, like windborne seeds in search of new ground. Will this place eventually seep into my bones, or will I always be an uncomfortable newcomer?

Last spring, a carpet of exotic tulips sprang up in the cemetery, sprinkling rainbow colors on the ground between the stones, beneath the ancient cedars. The living, the dead, the native, the introduced—all together, as if it had always been that way.

Rebel Yell in the Mall

—Susan Zakin

I used to fantasize about putting a personal ad in my local newspaper. "Rebel Girl Wants to Grow Up" would be the headline. I wasn't quite sure where to take it from there.

I never got up the nerve, but it occurred to me that I've gone ahead and, despite my best intentions, become a grown-up. This is the way I can tell: I have become a cash machine, mostly for large corporations.

Like most things, this is more obvious when you live in the desert. Usually things are visible here because there aren't a lot of trees to hide behind. In this case, it's because desert cities are the epitome of suburban sprawl. We drive everywhere. We shop at chain stores. We damn well better like it.

I'm a latecomer to malls. I arrived as a rugged individualist, rebelling against my East Coast prep school upbringing. I had rebelled on the East Coast, too, with some measure of success. Then I fell in love with emptiness, the open sea of the desert. It was a place where you stood up all alone and you could see for miles.

So I moved to the outskirts of Tucson, next door to a national park. In the intervening years, I became a cash machine.

It could have been when I signed up for an HMO—that's practically all we've got in Arizona—but I didn't notice anything until the HMO was bought out by a bigger HMO. The HMO raised the rates and doubled the price of prescriptions. By the way, it's Pacificare (Santa Ana, California), and their representatives are welcome to call me and explain why I should put up with this, besides the fact that most of the others are just as bad.

Or maybe I became a cash machine when Borders Books (Ann Arbor, Michigan) moved to town. A friend of mine called me, another mid-list author—that's what the industry calls us when our books don't really make any money, but we write good books, anyway. He spoke in a near-whisper: "There's a new bookstore on Oracle Road. It's a chain. And I like it."

Then Starbucks (famously Seattle) came. It was all over.

For instance, today I got in my pickup truck and drove twenty-three miles to see the doctor on the rich side of town where doctors like to practice. Later I went to Blimpie (Atlanta, Georgia), for which I have a sentimental childhood attachment. After achieving the requisite slight Blimpie nausea, I dropped $26.58 buying coffee, jam, Chai, and handmade tortillas at Trader Joe's (South Pasadena, California). You can get fresh tortillas in the barrio. But you know what? They're not as good as Trader Joe's; the barrio tortillas are made by machines.

Then I went to the Book Mark, which is Tucson's last independent general-interest bookstore. The Book Mark is going out of business, so I spent $57.21 buying books by local authors, most of which I can't find at the chains. Even with the going-out-of-business discount, I had to put them on my MasterCard (Wilmington, Delaware).

After that I went to the GKC Theater (Springfield, Illinois) and paid $1.75 to see *The Truman Show*. That movie explained everything. The recent sale of Ingram—a book distributor—to the giant Barnes & Noble conglomerate (New York, New York) woke me up to the fact that the industry in which I work is now the functional equivalent of an HMO. Writers are mere commodities, numbers on a spreadsheet. We write our life stories because we're too imaginatively bankrupt to come up with vital fiction. Once you've sold your life, what is left to sell? *The Truman Show* made it all clear. Jim Carrey—Truman—is an unwanted baby purchased by a corporation. The company sets up a safe, bland world for him. The only problem is that it's a phony world. Truman is a patsy for the corporation, which is making money from product placements in the TV show that is his life.

Truman escapes at the end, but it isn't so easy in real life. As I left the theater, I realized I was low on gas. I turned into the nearest Chevron station (San Francisco, California), whipped out my ATM card, gassed up—$11.27 plus the twenty-five-cent charge to my bank account with Norwest (San Francisco, California, too)—and headed home, back to my rugged individualist's life in the desert.

Actually, I don't know how much longer I can live here. I'm thinking of going to work for a corporation, too. The way things are going, I may not even have a choice.

Dodging Bumper Cars

—Auden Schendler

I learned to drive on the streets of Alphabet City in lower Manhattan. Moving west, I worried that I might lose the reflexes I honed dodging crack dealers and suicidal taxi drivers. No such luck. I commute on Colorado's Highway 82—the Roaring Fork Valley's proving ground for road ragers and budding stock-car drivers cutting their teeth on the commute to Aspen.

This place is not unique: The West's rural valleys are increasingly commuter thoroughfares, where bedroom communities feed service-economy hubs dozens of miles away. Former urbanites bring their road-warrior mentality, and one-time rural drivers are baptized in the killing fields. In Montana the bumper stickers read, "Pray for me: I drive Highway 93."

Many towns are dealing with crisis traffic and doing what they can to make life tolerable. Here, state troopers line the edges of the newly completed High Occupancy Vehicle (HOV) lane. They're waiting to pounce on violators: single drivers pilfering the free-flowing lane. If you get caught, there are no warnings; it's a sixty-five-dollar fine for first-time offenders.

The HOV lane adds new sport to a commute that's as close to combat as most of us will experience. There are intersections out of *The Dukes of Hazzard*, merges that thread between backhoes and Jersey barriers, lines and ruts that lead off into the brush. Often a driver will drift off—perhaps in a reverie of a better place—and lightly bump the car in front, which bumps the next car, creating a pulse in the traffic. I have seen people do nothing in response: Maybe the wave of minor collisions is comforting evidence there is life out there after all.

When the carpool lane first went in, there were letters in the paper from people so ingrained in the single-driver mentality that they spoke logical gobbledygook: "Obviously the HOV lane isn't working. I sat in traffic for an hour while people zipped past me. My tax dollars paid for the new lane and now I don't get to use it?" And this with a definition of "HOV"— two passengers—that would make hard-core Easterners snort. Still, the incentive is starting to work. Those who once scorned and feared hitchhikers now offer them coffee. Increasingly, commuters will do anything to be HOV-positive, including the ultimate sacrifice, the worst way to start your day: riding with somebody else.

It's not hard to understand the single-occupancy mentality. My friend Joe, an accountant, works in a basement in Aspen, commuting thirty miles from Carbondale. He rarely carpools and won't ride the bus. His two hours of sitting in traffic on the margins of the day are the only solitude he gets. With a thousand-dollar stereo and a collection of CDs to rival the local radio station, a plug of tobacco, and a quart of jet-fuel coffee, Joe promotes a kind of urban chemical meditation. He says, "I won't ride that goddamn bus. It's full of freaks. And some guy's always drinking grain alcohol next to me. I don't need that." Ask Joe for a ride and he winces.

My boss, on the other hand, carpools. While his wife drives, he gives advice on how to deal with the bottlenecks that occur at sections of the highway that haven't been two-laned: "Don't merge from the HOV lane until the last possible second. Cruise on the shoulder if you have to. Do the Miami merge—don't use the brakes." When he's not urging her on, he's screaming out the window at violators, reaching across to honk the horn and flip them off, giving the double thumbs up to the state troopers, who sometimes nod back wearily. When his wife tells him to calm down—it's not worth the pain!—he explains that he enjoys raging like this: It's how he likes to start the day.

One day, all of Highway 82 will be four lanes. Then, a commuter told me, the traffic will be gone. His evidence: When two lanes open to four on the commute home, the traffic eases up. But the completion of four lanes is ten years out, and analysts predict we'll need six by then. How can they be so sure? They've run the models—they're called Salt Lake, Seattle, Los Angeles.

I volunteer for a local ambulance and sometimes pull people from car wrecks. At one particularly nasty incident, I heard rumors from witnesses that the driver had tried to pass five or six cars at once and didn't seem to care there was oncoming traffic—he just floored it. I don't know if the story is true, but I believe it, since I've felt that kind of despair. After all, many Coloradans moved to the state to escape the East or West Coast, where traffic is just one of many horrors. To sit in traffic here must be the death of a dream.

Sometimes I float down the river in my kayak during rush hour. Bobbing on blue spring runoff, I am as relaxed as a monk. The rhythm of making eddy turns can vanquish an after-work headache. Up the steep rocky bank, commuters fester in gridlock. The contrast is so great I think it should produce light along the interface.

The Reluctant Landlord
—*Ed Quillen*

Time was, I'd gently correct people when they complimented me about how smart I was nearly a decade ago when I held onto an old house in a ramshackle Colorado mountain town.

In 1989, our daughters were turning into teenagers, and we wanted a bigger house. Half the town was for sale then, being as the mines and quarries had shut down, and so we got a good deal on a four-bedroom brick Victorian.

A good deal, but not an easy deal for us. We had to stretch for every nickel to make our move, and we planned to sell the old house and apply the proceeds to our new house. Thus, a rather dilapidated two-bedroom house went on the market for $30,000. The "For Sale" sign stayed there for two and a half years, without attracting any offers, even an insulting one.

Without much choice, we rented out the place until we could sell it. When we couldn't sell it, we adjusted to realty reality by taking it off the market and continuing our unplanned career move: landlording.

Back when everybody in town was poor, it was a pleasure. Our tenants took good care of the property, paid the rent promptly, and left the place spotless when it was time to move on. We preferred to rent to young working families at a rate below the market. We wanted to walk the talk that you hear in any socially conscious discussion of mountain-town economics about the shortage of affordable housing, the difficulty that employees have finding housing close to their work, the need for yards where children and pets can thrive.

Then a few People of Money discovered our town and began moving in. Realtors called with astonishing offers for that house they couldn't sell back when I desperately needed to sell it, and that rise in demand meant a rise in market price, for rental or for sale. So we did raise the rent a few dollars a month every time a tenant moved on, but we still kept the rent below market. We rented to people with pets and children and tobacco habits, and we were understanding when a tenant said he might be a few days late with the rent.

That made for a pleasant relationship in 1992. In 1998, after the town got favorable mention in everything from *Outside* and *Sunset* to *Mountain Bike Monthly* and *The 100 Best Small Art Towns in America*, it has become an impossible relationship.

I can't put my finger on exactly what's changed, but it's probably related to what I heard from a longtime Aspen resident one night in a Gunnison bar. He bemoaned how "we've developed an upper class and a servant class. Before the big money arrived in the eighties, you might sit down and drink with the waiter after dinner—he might well have had a Ph.D., that sort of thing—but that doesn't happen now."

This isn't Aspen (not even close, except in the summer when the pass is open), but the dynamics seem to be evolving toward the same end: class division. And I'm stuck in an uncomfortable position.

After spending the better part of a fortnight, and filling a two-yard dumpster three times, to clean up after the last tenant—who always seemed to have money for new trucks and the latest in Wal-Mart household junk, but who never paid his rent on time—I find myself less interested in Big Bill Haywood and *Mother Jones* and too often sounding like a member of the local Republican central committee.

"What's with these people?" I mutter to myself. "I tried to be fair, and the SOB just took advantage of me." The first time or two this happened, I felt it was a variety of karmic justice: What went around when I was a rowdy young tenant came around when I was a landlord.

But that's over. Now I think how much easier my life would be if the next tenants had steady jobs and no pets, especially dogs that dig holes in the lawn and cats that confuse floors with litter boxes. Maybe no children, especially brats that shoot BBs into the walls. And without common habits, since wine stains are impossible to remove from carpets, and cigarette burns are even harder to remove from countertops.

In other words, I wouldn't rent to myself—no steady job but with several pets and children and vices. Even weirder, this bizarre market allows me to charge a rent that I couldn't afford now.

Hypocrisy? Sloth, because I just want the money every month and don't want to have to labor for it? Am I honorably protecting an investment for the continuing benefit of my family? Or is this class warfare, with me now standing uncomfortably at the capitalist barricades?

No answer appears, except the impossible one of turning the clock back a decade, to when we were all poor here and landlords and tenants weren't automatic enemies.

2. Myth Busting

Saint Contrary: John Wesley Powell
—William deBuys

If the American West were to adopt a secular, faulted, feet-of-clay patron saint, John Wesley Powell, whose March 24 birthday just passed, would be the man.

Powell, who died in 1902, epitomized grit and courage, qualities the West likes to honor. He lost an arm at Shiloh while commanding a battery at the heart of the hottest fighting. Then, his stump barely healed, he fought on through Vicksburg and Atlanta. Undeterred, he was the first to descend a thousand white-water miles of the grand Colorado River, and having done that and barely survived, he promptly did it a second time.

Powell was a scientist, geologist, geographer, and ethnographer. He prowled the Four Corners backcountry of the so-called Wild West in its wildest post–Civil War days, and he did not carry a gun. He believed the best way to get along with the region's Native people was to show you meant no harm—and to mean none.

He founded the Bureau of American Ethnology and sponsored hundreds of research investigations of enduring value, on the premise that Native cultures demanded study and understanding. Having led one of the four great surveys of the American West, he also posed—and largely answered—the fundamental questions about how the Colorado Plateau was carved to its present form.

A student of the West could push all that aside and still have reason to honor J. W. Powell. Although his vision for the region ultimately failed, many westerners today might find it agreeable. Powell was a bureaucrat, but he did not believe in the bureaucratization of the West. He believed the federal government's role was to inventory and organize the West, then to release its lands and resources to the control of watershed commonwealths, which were to be locally and democratically governed.

Although Powell's plan for western settlement suffered total defeat, it is not hard to understand what he had in mind. His commonwealths were much like irrigation districts: Their first task was to regulate and apportion water for agricultural and domestic use. At a local or at most regional level, they would construct the dams, canals, and drains necessary for development of small-scale, family-run farms.

Unlike today's irrigation districts, however, Powell's commonwealths would also have been responsible for management of their watersheds' uplands. Powell believed that self-interest was the key to good stewardship: No sanely governed commonwealth would abuse its uplands lest the quality and quantity of its water decline.

One reason he opposed the creation of a national forestry service (and aroused the ire of many conservationists of his day) was that he feared the erosion of a local sense of responsibility. Another was his conviction that no federal agency could long remain immune from political (read: industrial) influence. Given the West's history of clear-cut forests and disenfranchised local communities, you can't say Powell was wrong.

Powell's commonwealths would have managed the forests for both timber and water. They would have regulated grazing, imposing limits on the unbridled exploitation of rangelands a good half century or so before the too late and too weak Taylor Grazing Act came into play.

Today, the public lands are largely governed by administrative pyramids whose tops are lost in the cloudy altitudes of Washington. Much of what passes for democracy is simply the struggle of competing coalitions to control those peaks. Powell's plan would have decapitated the pyramids, forcing decisions to be made in a local arena of face-to-face community contact.

The results would have been far from perfect, but they would have been diverse. Different commonwealths would have taken different approaches. The rate of trial-and-error experimentation would likely have been high, and the rate of learning, one hopes, also high. One wonders how things might have been.

But Powell was soundly defeated. Prospective homesteaders did not like the idea of surrendering the public domain to the collective control of commonwealths. Timber interests did not want farmers in charge of the forests. Entrepreneurs did not care to answer to anybody. In the end, most folks agreed that the wide-open, free-for-all rush to riches that has always characterized western settlement was pretty much okay.

Powell's importance was not that he was right; his plan would have righted some wrongs but created a hothouse for growing others. It was that he saw the West on its own terms, as a place that needed to grow its own institutions and wrestle with its problems in its own homegrown way.

A hundred years ago, Powell made nearly everyone uneasy. His thinking was too bold, too unconventional. He challenged people. Same thing today. He still doesn't fit, still makes people uneasy. Good for him. Good for us if we listen to him.

It's a Good Day to Be Indigenous
—*Stephen Lyons*

From this moment on kindly refer to my family as "indigenous" or, if you prefer, "First Peoples." With the discovery of what could be my long-lost European relative—Kennewick Man—it's time to respect my elders.

Kennewick Man, found in 1996 on the banks of the Columbia River near the town of the same name in Washington State, is alleged to have "European features" and is 9,300 years old, thus predating the initial arrival of Native Americans to the area. In fact, only one set of bones in the United States is older: Senator Strom Thurmond's.

When forensic anthropologist Jim Chatters briefly examined Kennewick Man, he announced to the world that our ancient guy resembled *Star Trek: the Next Generation* actor Patrick Stewart. But what other clues led Chatters to his controversial determination that this bag of bones was non-Indian? Perhaps it was the Timex watch, the plastic Big Gulp cup from 7-Eleven, or the Denver Broncos warm-up jacket. Judging by the rampant development in the American West, probably any early Europeans were real-estate developers—"Century 21 Men."

Chatters's speculation has triggered an avalanche of criticism, some from other scientists but mostly from a confederation of Northwest tribes who do not want to lose their sovereignty or change the tried and true story that Native Americans arrived first and then we came and screwed up everything. The Confederation wants Kennewick Man returned to them so he and any further scientific specimens can be buried in an undisclosed location, thus preventing any holes being opened into their belief systems.

Tribes cite the 1990 federal Native American Graves Protection and Repatriation Act that requires skeletons found in Native American areas to be turned over to the tribes. However, the skeleton must be a proven descendant, and back in the days of Kennewick Man no one kept detailed records.

After pleading his case before the House Resources Committee, Armand Minthorn, leader of Oregon's Umatilla Tribe, said to *The Seattle Times*, "We are not worried that study of the remains will change history, or cause us to lose our standing in history. We already know what happened 10,000 years ago. We know we have always been there."

Chatters countered, "We're seeing a real extremism developing here. The tribes basically are saying that they are in control of all human history in North America. They have always been here, and there are to be no more questions asked."

Chatters reminds one of a modern-day version of Italian astronomer Galileo, and the tribes are in the unfamiliar position of representing the status quo, the Church. Only 368 years ago, Galileo was forced by Rome to deny the truth—that the earth and all the planets revolve around the sun. In the 1600s his heretical views were too risky to an entire religious belief system. If Chatters's assumption is correct, Native Americans may have to rewrite their own history, and the odds of that happening are the same as of Kennewick Man suddenly rising from his Tupperware coffin to perform an Irish jig.

To prevent any of the above from happening, I've come to the rescue with some revisionist history: A handful of restless Europeans arrived in the Northwest 9,300 years ago but soon left because someone thought he had left a fire burning back home. All except Kennewick Man, who was a poet and not well regarded. He was lying on his back watching cloud formations and composing a long-winded essay about the Missoula Floods when the rest of the clan ditched him. A saber-toothed tiger came along, and the rest is ancient history.

Or we can just call it a tie. We all arrived about the same time, give or take a thousand years, and most of us hate icy roads.

At the end of October, Kennewick Man was moved under tight security to the Burke Museum at the University of Washington in Seattle, where he will rest while the legal battle continues. Before the move, an exhaustive inventory of the skeleton was performed by a team of researchers. Chatters was not invited to take part—maybe it was the Patrick Stewart remark.

While we await the archaeological verdict, I'm going to work on my new indigenous attitude. After 9,000 years of bad press, I think I deserve some compensation. I want a large tract of land. I want a culture that doesn't worship minivans. I want to play basketball with Sherman Alexie. I want the rest of you to copy my rituals, commercialize my culture, and romanticize my every twitch. Now, about those casino profits?

Cannibalizing a Sacred Belief
—*Art Goodtimes*

Good guys. Bad guys. It used to be pretty clear which side was which. When I was a kid back in the straight-arrow fifties, I knew that the Lone Ranger wore the white hat. He was on the side of justice, law, and order.

In the topsy-turvy sixties, as I learned how the West was really won, Tonto traded places with his masked compatriot and Columbus became the black-hatted villain.

Now, after reading Christy Turner's new book, *Man Corn: Cannibalism and Violence in the Prehistoric American Southwest* (University of Utah Press, 1998), I'm not so sure who's good and who's bad.

Man Corn is a translation of the Nahuatl (Aztec) word *tlacatlaolli*, which refers to a "sacred meal of sacrificed human meat, cooked with corn." What Turner proposes is that the great Chacoan culture we've long celebrated for its architectural, agricultural, and cultural sophistication may also have been a society riddled with terror, violence, and even cannibalism.

Turner, a physical anthropologist specializing in dental morphology, first stumbled into the skeletal record of a Hopi massacre while he was examining Anasazi teeth at Flagstaff's Museum of Northern Arizona. This initial discovery prompted Turner to reexamine some seventy-two Anasazi sites where cannibalism might have occurred. Of those, thirty-eight show clear evidence of cannibalism, while most of the rest suggest extreme violence and mutilation. Turner also examined a collection of 870 Anasazi skeletons at the Museum of Northern Arizona in Flagstaff and found that 8 percent, or one in every twelve, showed the telltale marks of cannibalism—burn patterns on the skull, perimortem breaks, anvil abrasions, sucked-out bone marrow, polished and beveled bone tips (from having been stirred in a rough ceramic pot).

Lots of Turner's detractors have proposed alternate interpretations of the bone record, and many have criticized Turner for not working with the Puebloan peoples and of being insensitive to the negative political ramifications of his findings.

For years it seemed as though Turner's thesis was built as much on conjecture as on irrefutable evidence. Then in the early 1990s, a contract archaeology firm excavated a group of prehistoric sites at the base of Sleeping Ute Mountain on the Colorado–New Mexico border and came up with a smoking gun.

At an otherwise unremarkable site along Cowboy Wash, known as 5MT 10010, the archaeologists found three kivas. The first contained a pile of chopped-up human bones that appeared to have been tossed down into the room from outside. The second contained the bones from five individuals who'd been roasted and eaten, along with a butchering tool kit—ax, hammerstones, and two large flakes with razor-thin cutting edges. When analyzed, these tested positive for human blood. The third kiva contained coprolite, or fossilized human excrement, directly atop the ashes of the central hearth. As archaeologist Brian Billman theorized, "After the fire had gone cold, someone had squatted over this hearth and defecated into it."

Later lab analyses proved conclusively that the coprolite showed the presence of human myoglobin protein. No mistake. This was human cannibalism—and a kind of terrorism calculated to inspire fear in all who came near this site.

Still I can't quite accept this changed picture of the master builders of Casa Rinconada and the paleo-astronomers of Fajada Butte. For years I'd insisted on calling them "Hisatsinom," the Hopi word for "ancient ones," and disdained the common term "Anasazi," a Navajo or Diné word for "ancient enemies."

But now I'm not so sure "ancient enemies" isn't the best term, after all, to describe these mysterious ancestors. Maybe the Diné had good reason for their aversion to Anasazi sites, their deep-rooted fear of what, it turns out, may have been a culture gone quite awry.

No longer can I put Chaco Canyon on some kind of ancient Parthenon-like pedestal and see in it an ideal society lost, a primitive utopian vision that we need to work back toward as we step into the future. Instead, I am left with the haunting realization that good and evil, human achievement and human tragedy, cultural marvels and cultural misdeeds are inseparable parts of the circle of life as we know it. And as the Anasazi knew it.

Even today, to walk the Beauty Way, as the Puebloan peoples and the Diné still believe, is not to stand in the light or revel in the dark but to walk the path between light and dark, the one balancing the other.

It's sobering to realize that, at certain times in the history of all peoples, balance can be lost and a society—even one revered like the Anasazi—can be plunged into the terror of a Hitler, a Pol Pot.

Honoring the First Discoverers
—Dan Oko

As the Lewis and Clark Expedition crossed the Bitterroot Mountains from Montana into Idaho in 1805, members of the Nez Perce tribe spied on the group. The Indians didn't know what to make of the blue-eyed, wild-haired American soldiers and initially thought to kill them and take their supplies. It was only through the intervention of a Nez Perce woman named Watkuweis that the famed explorers were spared.

Meriwether Lewis, William Clark, and their men spent a week among the Nez Perce, recovering from their arduous journey. All the while they would have been easy prey. But Watkuweis, having been a slave of the Blackfeet and white traders—her name means "Returned from a Far Country"—told her people that the whites had been kinder to her than the Blackfeet. "These are the people who helped me," she is reported to have said. "Do them no harm." So the explorers were allowed to continue on their way to the Pacific Ocean and to take their place in American history as heroes of the first degree.

The story of Watkuweis is known by many Indian people, who correctly point out that the tale reflects a chapter in the opening of the American frontier often passed over in favor of a more gallant portrait of Lewis and Clark. The author Stephen Ambrose recounted this "lost" bit of history in his 1996 best-seller *Undaunted Courage*, stating flatly that "the United States owed more to the Nez Perce for their restraint than it ever acknowledged." Even so, despite the buzz attending the upcoming Lewis and Clark bicentennial, it seems unlikely that most Americans will learn of the crucial role the Nez Perce and other tribal people played in the Corps of Discovery reaching the Pacific.

Currently, planners from St. Louis to the Oregon coast are trying to figure out the potential impact of millions of visitors on communities along the Lewis and Clark Trail in the year 2003. Although nobody knows exactly how many travelers will attempt to retrace the steps taken by the expedition, the U.S.D.A. Forest Service, U.S. Bureau of Land Management, and agencies of various states are developing strategies to contend with increased tourism. Montana, Oregon, and other states have also convened special commissions to get a handle on gains and losses posed by the coming celebration.

With the bicentennial four years away, many view the countdown to the millennium as merely a pit stop before modern-day adventurers arrive to explore the route from the Great Plains to the Pacific. In some places, anticipation of the bicentennial, which could run through 2006, is marked by the hope that credit-card–carrying travelers will drop enough dough to rejuvenate sagging economies dependent on tourist dollars. As these virtual hordes amass around the edges of local imaginations, archaeologists and others work to identify the places where Lewis and Clark once slept. These researchers hope to log as much data as possible before visitors forever alter the relatively untrammeled character of such places.

Of course, another group of westerners has a different stake in this commemoration. For Native Americans, whose ancestors traversed this continent well ahead of Lewis and Clark, the coming bicentennial is fraught with psychic and cultural risks. Not only is the Corps of Discovery viewed as a harbinger of the Indian Wars, but the coming celebration marks the potential for a continued trampling of culturally significant sites that, in many cases, have already been exploited by treasure hunters and tourists looking to own a piece of history.

In cases where these spots represent a spiritual heritage still alive, such actions carry the same impact as defacing chapel walls and leaving garbage in the aisles of churches. More to the point, the desecration of Native American cultural sites perpetuates racist beliefs and actions that have long plagued this country.

By remembering the active role Native Americans played in helping Lewis and Clark succeed, those responsible for planning the bicentennial can raise awareness of the rich multicultural heritage that imbues the places many of us today call home. As I heard a teacher from Montana's Flathead Reservation put it recently, "I challenge all of you to have the utmost dignity and to do something good with something that was very bad for a lot of people. This [the bicentennial] is an opportunity for healing, for acknowledging debt. It's an opportunity for all of us to regain our full humanity."

Harley-Burly

—John Clayton

Once upon a time, I'm sure, the arrival of hundreds of bikers in your town was intimidating. Now it's somewhat comical, as bald, beer-bellied men creak off their motorcycles and wallow around in their virginal leather sweatpants. These are not thugs. They're a walking definition of "midlife crisis."

I've just lived through an ultimate "New West" affair, something called "The Iron Horse Rodeo: An All-Harley Event."

The centerpiece of the weekend was literally a biker rodeo, with games of skill: going fast or slow around obstacles or grabbing things from the air. There was also a poker run through the surrounding mountain landscape, a wet T-shirt contest, and a street dance featuring (of all things) a reggae band.

Several waitresses commented on how polite and generous they were. Good tippers. Given the price of a new Harley these days, that shouldn't be surprising: Most of them are rich. They're professionals with disposable income, and the throttle of their engines sounds to many local merchants like money.

With downtown parking spaces marked off "For Motorcycles Only," and with the fully costumed drivers of those bikes wandering everywhere and congregating on every corner, our town had been transformed into a movie set for an alien planet. And yet, when you looked closer, the sight had familiar trappings. It was the Old West reincarnated. The bikers wore enough metal and leather to make you wonder how mining and ranching could be considered declining industries, and the infuriating whine of their motors reminded me of a chain saw, although without the subsequent thwap of tree against earth—or actual work being performed.

The annual weekend's original organizers, I'm sure, got a kick out of reinventing the rodeo as a biker event. As it grew, they may have also appreciated the irony of what used to be "outlaw bikers" now being welcomed as "economic development." But it didn't strike me until this year—when the name was changed from the "All-Harley Rodeo" to the "Iron Horse Rodeo"—how deep the organizers' mythological ambitions were. I mean, isn't "Iron Horse" supposed to be the railroad? It made me realize how empty our old myths are. Savvy marketers can portray bikes as both horses and trains, can portray their riders as both cowpokes and outlaws.

This is the New West. Take a myth, an image; twist it around to fit your product; and make a lot of money. It's not just bikers. Everyone claims to be a cowboy these days. Telecommuters, miners, movie stars. How are yuppies tied to their computers, wage slaves running machines in underground tunnels, and insecure millionaires who tote around their personal espresso machines similar to people who herd cattle from horseback? That's irrelevant. The point is they want to believe it, and you can make money pretending to agree with them.

People interested in environmental politics mistakenly believe that the New West is about their issues. I've got bad news for you folks: I didn't hear any of the Harley riders talking about the demise of extractive-based industries or the expansion of telecommunications infrastructure or incentives for habitat protection on private lands. Mostly they talked about their bikes.

Because that's all the New West is: a place where you can buy whatever image you've always dreamed about or seen on a big screen. Whether you want to be an "outlaw biker" or a "carefree retiree" or a "rock climber," the first and most important step is to buy a T-shirt. Luxury log cabins. Exclusive hunting preserves. Fur-trapper rendezvous reenactments. Helicopter skiing. All of them take nineteenth-century myths of open, rugged lands, dress them up with twenty-first–century amenities, and sell the images to rich people.

Thinking about all this started getting me pretty depressed. Then, being a refugee myself, I realized the flip side: At least the West still has myths to misappropriate. Let's face it, Harleys invading Connecticut just wouldn't have much to do.

The funny thing was, despite the awful noise and the stench of burned rubber, despite the bikers' apparent sexism, their ridiculous get-ups, and their confused reinterpretations of history, I liked them. In a society where we suffer from an excess of luxury and a dearth of ways to put it in wider perspective, the all-Harley rodeo participants embodied a West that is still the sort of place where we see life in terms of myths.

A Woman's Secret for Survival on the Ranch

—Linda Hasselstrom

Ranch women work hard, and complex problems tie them to the world's economy. But every country woman you see in the newspaper or on TV is smiling. A big, toothy smile of pure joy, even if she's not wearing makeup and her hair is blowing and a cow has just kicked her. Are they all a little short on candlepower?

No; we know *the secret.* We're not supposed to tell, because we like the country uncrowded. Promise not to move out here?

Get a 115-pound woman her own coveralls, overshoes, and a tractor or horse, and she can do anything a man can do. And she'll do less cooking, cleaning, and canning.

In the old days, farm wives wore frilly dresses in tidy houses, could produce a nine-course dinner for six men with fifteen minutes' warning, and were still expected to swoon if lightning struck within six miles.

Many a farm husband didn't notice that in an average day his wife picked and canned twelve bushels of tomatoes; hoed, weeded, and watered the garden; gathered eggs; butchered a hen for Sunday dinner; shoveled the chicken house clean; and did laundry. He might notice if she didn't whisk on a clean apron, smile, and serve the steak and spuds. Without complaint.

Some farm husbands began to think of women as fragile creatures too delicate to do outdoor farm or ranch labor, and maybe not quite smart enough either. Then came the mechanical revolution, followed closely by liberation. Women, said new scientific studies, can learn how to drive a tractor, plow a straight furrow, mow a field.

Smart farm and ranch wives didn't waste a minute. Jerking off their aprons, they grabbed an old shirt and hat and offered to help with the outside work. Before you could say "Old McDonald had a farm," they were humming to themselves in fresh air as they loosened a rusty nut on the sickle bar or wiped grease out of their eyes as they crawled under the John Deere.

At dinnertime, they strolled arm in arm with their husbands into the house, washed side by side at the sink, and then—then they *both* went into the kitchen. After all, she'd been outside all morning helping with *his* work.

We soon learned that the average farmer had skills never before imagined. He *could* slice lettuce into a bowl and dump salad dressing over it without cutting his finger more than once. He could peel potatoes, although he was wasteful, and figure out whether the peelings belonged in the recycling pail, the can for burnable waste, the one for chicken scraps, or the compost bucket. He could even bring in the sun tea and pry ice cube trays out of the refrigerator.

A new day dawned in the country: A husband and wife sat down *together* at the dinner table, instead of the wife pouring coffee and warming up potatoes while the husband and children ate. New topics of conversation opened. A wife who has mowed a hundred acres of hay may have noticed a fence that needs fixing or seen the bulls getting in with the cows at an inopportune time. The children may remark on how very well-muscled Mom's arms are, ushering in a new age of peace and harmony based on respect for superior strength.

When the woman goes to town for spare parts, she can stride up to the counter, slap down a chunk of cold iron, and instead of whispering to a sneering clerk about "replacement for the thingamajig," confidently ask for "a new set of rings for this hydraulic unit; it's a 1972 Farmhand."

Life takes on new meaning for the woman who has opened communication with a tractor. Once she masters driving a tractor around a field in ever-decreasing concentric squares, she has acres of time to think; she might even write poetry. In the house, she never sat down without darning socks.

On a tractor, with half her attention on machinery noises and smells, she can devote the other half to more important things. Are her children getting spoiled? With Mother working outside, they'll take more responsibility. The Pilgrims said, "He who doesn't work, doesn't eat"—an excellent motto for child rearing.

No longer will the trip to the sale ring be a boring afternoon. She's mowed hay and pitched it to those steers, given them shots. Their sale price is suddenly translated into payment she gets for her work, not just an abstract figure to cover food and school shoes.

Yes, she'll still have housework to do or supervise, but suddenly those chores will become simply jobs to finish, not her whole existence. And while she does dishes—and her husband or children dry—she'll have new things to talk about: the eagle that swooped out of the field with a snake in his claws, the fawn she didn't mow into this afternoon. She'll see more of the life cycle—and realize doing dishes isn't part of it.

February Is the Cruelest Month
—*Penelope Reedy*

Before cars and plowed roads, it was worse, they say—deadly, in fact. Now we have "communication" devices to assuage our loneliness: telephones, email, four-wheel-drive vehicles, television, and more, but even so, cabin fever still affects a strong segment of the American West's rural population.

Humans are social, political animals (or so said Plato), a philosophy that conflicts sharply with the western American desire to live alone in an isolated mountain cabin as far from civilization as possible.

"Where you can't hear the hum of a highway or see another person in any direction for miles," said my father, my grandfather, my ex-husband, my sons. My summer vacations with these men were always lonely. I wanted to meet new people, talk, hear how they lived, what they thought about, but if another group of campers on the South Boise or Little Smokey Rivers came within sight of our camp, we packed up and moved on. Outsiders were the enemy infringing upon our private wilderness.

"These mountains were ours, all ours," said my Aunt Nellie about her courtship years with my uncle, Frank Croner, in the 1920s. My preschool daughters and I had taken her for a drive down memory lane in the Sawtooth Mountains a few short years after Uncle Frank died.

Theodore Kaczynski holed up alone in a cabin in rural Montana while scheming and manufacturing bombs to take his revenge on society. The Unabomber, we're told, fits a dangerous sociopathic profile; but his landscape is familiar territory to westerners; it came as no surprise to us that he'd sought out an isolated cabin.

Henry David Thoreau, for all his wonderful writing about spending a year in his tiny cabin on the shores of Walden Pond, was also a bit of a nut, I've heard. Other residents of Concord, Massachusetts, including transcendentalist Ralph Waldo Emerson, were not always happy to see him arrive at their doors at mealtimes with a new cause dripping maniacally from his sleeve.

Less famous products of isolation include a pair of men who lived up Soldier Creek north of Fairfield, Idaho, circa 1895. As a small child, my stepfather's mother watched her father greet one of these men leading a horse into the barnyard. The body of the man's partner was draped over the back of the horse.

"I shot the son of a bitch," the man said.

The pair had spent the winter alone, holed up in a tiny cabin under deep snows.

My Uncle Frank, a former Fairfield town marshall in the 1920s (he was born in 1901), told me about "the spring fights," how tension would build up all winter among Camas Prairie dwellers. As soon as the snow thawed in April, when farmers could get to town again, they'd meet on Main Street or at the town saloon and beat the pulp out of each other.

Today in the western Rockies, February is still the cruelest month. If a teacher or other newcomer is going to be run out of town, the sentiments building toward the expulsion originate in February over coffee klatches at the cafe, during downtime in the school bus barn, or over Sunday dinner after a rousing sermon on sin and the evils of insidious secular humanism.

In February, the promise of spring spars cruelly with the calendar. Seed catalogs arrive with colored photos of hope. Most plants in the catalogs won't even survive on the high western prairies, but we order them anyway. This year will be different.

In February a sadistic beauty sparkles in the frosty morning air. A lone coyote, his hair tipped in frost, moves silently across a grain field. The family dog bristles his own frost-tipped ruff. A pile of books set out for winter reading by the fire lies barely touched. Where does the time go?

Feed the cows; gather eggs before they freeze solid; see if the car will start; scan the horizon anxiously for the postman.

Winter, just keeping warm is tiring; we go to bed at six, get up at eleven. There's only so much fudge, popcorn, and Monopoly a family can handle after dark.

"If you chew with your mouth open one more time, I'll . . . ."

Come March, we quietly begin discarding the relief maps we made out of our fingernail clippings. We no longer recall the obsession that drove us to design them. We build fires on the first patch of bare ground that emerges in the yard, toast marshmallows, watch the first Canada geese and sandhill cranes return to the river bottoms south of the ranch house.

This year, I'm planting grape vines.

The Shooting That Made Guns Real
—*Jim Stiles*

I was ten years old and my brother was just seven when we watched my best friend, Timmy Caldwell, shoot his brother with a rifle. With cold deliberate aim, Timmy leveled the Winchester .30/.30 lever-action carbine at five-year-old Brad Caldwell and calmly squeezed the trigger.

Little Brad fell backward, clutched his chest, and crumpled to the ground, his face a mask of agony and stunned disbelief. He twitched a couple of times and then lay still in our very own front yard.

Timmy stepped to his brother's side, not a hint of emotion on his face, and bent down for a closer look. Finally he said, "That was the phoniest dying scene I've ever watched. Get up, Brad, and we'll do it again."

Brad opened his eyes and started to giggle. "What d'ya mean, Timmy? I thought I died pretty good."

When I was a kid, we shot each other all the time. I cannot imagine the number of times I died of gunshot wounds between the ages of eight and twelve. We called it "playing guns." We'd say, "Hey, you guys, you wanna go play guns?" Later we'd decide which armed conflict to play guns in. We went through phases: World War II worked well for a while. The Alamo was always a winner. Playing gangsters allowed us to assume the roles of real crooks. I always got stuck playing Baby Face Nelson, however, which stigmatized me to this very day.

A lot more than playing guns did. It's odd. My friends and I grew up with television, religiously watched one shoot 'em up western and cops 'n robbers show after another, went out and recreated all those acts of violence on a regular basis, but none of us ever thought to get our fathers' guns or look for real ammunition. We had our problems in school and got mad at our friends and teachers. But it never occurred to us to shoot them to death.

What's the difference? Why are children shooting each other nowadays? And their parents? And their teachers? Child psychologists tell us these kids are affected by the media violence that pervades our lives, but child psychologists have been saying that for thirty years.

If you watch the way death is portrayed on television and in the movies today, compared to death scenes when I was a kid, you might find a clue. The graphic nature of the violence is the difference, and the irony is that it took a graphic death in real life to change the way Hollywood portrayed death on the screen.

Find a good Bogart film from the forties or any western from the fifties and watch the bad guys get shot by Bogie or Roy or Gene and, even in the most serious of films, what you will see is cinematic death that is almost comical. There were no bloodstains. We knew the actors would get back up again as soon as the director said "Cut." So while we played guns and riddled each other mercilessly with "hot lead," we never took death seriously or the notion that we could cause death ourselves.

Violent death became very real to me in November 1963. On a Friday afternoon, we learned that President Kennedy had been assassinated in Dallas. I can still remember the day and the way I felt and walking home from school and watching the story all weekend on television. We learned that an amateur photographer had filmed the assassination and that *Life* magazine would publish each frame of the film in its next issue.

When the magazine arrived, my brother and I searched for and found the pictures. We studied each frame as the limousine crept slowly down Elm Street, disappeared briefly behind a highway sign, and then reemerged in the bright Dallas sun.

It was as we had always imagined being shot was supposed to look. You see the president clutching his throat, slumping, and falling slightly forward and toward his wife. Just like in the movies. Then we turned the page. In frame 313, the president's head was suddenly obscured by a bright red mass of color. Jeff and I looked at each other quizzically: Was this some imperfection in the processing, we wondered?

It wasn't. It was John Kennedy's head shot to pieces. And it was our introduction to the real world of violent death. Two days later the president's accused assassin was shot to death on live television—the first nationally televised murder in history. How could Hollywood top that? It has been trying ever since.

Today's make-believe violence is so incredibly realistic, we no longer have any doubts about what real violence looks like. In fact, Hollywood has finally made real violence look tame. Now children understand the reality of violent death; what they cannot grasp is its permanence.

Except, perhaps, for those who experience violent death directly, such as the Columbine High School students in Littleton, Colorado. It's a hard way to learn. One can only hope that their grief, seen by millions on television and in newspapers, will seem more real than Hollywood.

Why I Still Love Guns

—*Rocky Barker*

In the wake of the tragic shootings in Littleton and other places, it has been difficult for people like me to express themselves publicly without immediately drawing the ire of usually moderate folk.

You see, I love guns.

My dad was a collector for as long as I can remember. Except for working on the farm, most of the time I spent alone with him—what people today call quality time—was spent roaming gun shows or driving to some distant gun shop to look for a bargain. Dad, a marine in Korea, has a taste for military weapons, especially Springfields, named for the armory in Massachusetts. Over the years he has owned everything from Springfields dating back to the Civil War to versions built for soldiers of his generation.

I share neither his military background nor his interest in collecting. I do share his love of hunting and sporting arms. It always seemed to me that guns were tools that needed to be used. I like the feel of a well-balanced shotgun in my hands. In these times of political correctness and polarized debates over gun control and crime, you don't often read much about the joy of bringing a Winchester Model 12 shotgun to the shoulder, or the smooth action of an old Parker double barrel.

If you do, you have to wade through all kinds of ideological discussion about the Second Amendment. When I want to talk about guns, the only ideological debate I care about is whether big calibers are better for hunting big game than smaller, faster rounds. I don't want to hear about Charleton Heston and Idaho's Senator Larry Craig. I want to talk about Jack O'Connor and Elmer Keith.

For those of you who didn't grow up with your face buried in *Outdoor Life* or *Field & Stream*, O'Connor and Keith were gun experts. They weren't just gun *experts*. They were *the* gun experts.

I don't have to tell people in Salmon, Idaho, who Elmer Keith was. He lived on a ranch in North Fork and started his long career in guns as a guide in the Middle Fork country. He took the prolific western writer Zane Grey hunting for deer in 1931. He wrote hundreds of articles and nine books. Keith helped create one of the finest rifles ever made, the Winchester Model 70 (pre-1964, of course). He developed the handgun calibers .357 magnum, .41 magnum, and .44 magnum, with which Clint Eastwood made his day.

Keith was a plain-speaking former cowboy in a ten-gallon hat. He was the primary advocate for using the biggest caliber possible. When asked once whether a caliber was too large, he is said to have remarked, "You mean it'll kill too dead?"

But you never heard him advocating hunting with machine guns.

O'Connor, often topped by a fedora, was more refined than the gritty Salmon cowboy. He grew up in Arizona but later moved to Lewiston, Idaho. He favored flat-shooting moderate calibers like the .270 and 30/06 (that's thirty-ought-six for those of you who don't handle guns).

What I didn't learn about ballistics, shooting, and gun care from my dad I learned from reading Keith, O'Connor, and another Idahoan, Clyde Ormond. Ormond, a retired high school principal from Rigby, taught me and thousands of other young outdoorsmen the basics of hunting and living in the outdoors in his many articles and books.

It saddens me as much as the next person to see that today many young people are more interested in the basics of bomb making than in how to stalk a deer. Most of the advances in weapons technology have revolved around making guns more effective killing machines by putting out more rounds faster in lighter and lighter packages, like the Uzi. Thankfully, sporting arms have not changed much, and I hope they don't.

The utilitarian elegance of sporting arms can't hide the fact that they are killing machines just like their assault-weapon cousins. The object of their use is to kill game as quickly, efficiently, and mercifully as possible. That has always placed more responsibility on the shooter than on the gun.

I no longer go to gun shows, and I don't keep grenades under my bed for protection as one of my dad's friends used to do. I lean toward the civility of a well-built ailling, a double-barreled shotgun with a rifle barrel underneath favored by European hunters. I'd rather be in a duck blind than on an urban shooting range.

Do I have a right to own guns? I'll leave deciding that up to the Supreme Court. I do know that my world would be far less rich without the tradition and link to the land they have brought me.

Flower Power for the Armed West

—Penelope Reedy

In the 1969 film classic *Easy Rider*, when two rednecks pulled shotguns off their pickup's gun rack and blew Billy and Wyatt off their chrome-plated choppers into oblivion, the western American myth of guns equaling freedom was blown away, too.

Never again could American westerners sleep comfortably under the illusion that most of us embrace similar traditional values. The black hats and the white hats of our mythology are no longer distinguishable.

With a hippie heart searching for peace and meaning in nature, I left New York City in 1970, a week after the Kent State massacre, and traveled to Camas County, Idaho, my father's birthplace. A year later, I married a cattle rancher. I went from marching in antiwar demonstrations to riding in a pickup truck with a fully stocked gun rack and cruising the high western prairies of my ancestors.

Camas Prairie is where my grandfather served as a teacher, probate judge, and prosecuting attorney. He was said to be a quiet man, having raised six sons and one daughter, all with the "burden" of an hysterical wife.

In the 1970s, I told myself my hippie years were little more than immature ramblings, that I had reformed, or returned to center, by marrying an ultraconservative rancher.

"He's not like them," I told myself.

But the gap between us widened as the years wore on.

I bought books; my husband threatened to burn them. I wanted rambling gardens, friends for dinner, conversation and dancing; he insisted everything be planted in straight lines and piled stove wood on my flower gardens. I discouraged my city friends from visiting because I had grown afraid of what he might do.

There were guns hidden all over our house. He shot the "too many" puppies in the driveway just as the school bus full of kids arrived. He shot a stray dog in the yard while drunk, unconcerned where our four children were at the time or what their feelings might be.

When our daughter was sleepwalking one night, his first response was to grab the .38 magnum in a drawer by the bed.

To keep me and our children in line, he made occasional dramatic exits, packing a holstered pistol implying suicide.

When his friends' wives threatened to leave their husbands, the first thing the men did was bring their guns to our house to keep the women from selling them. "Our" guns disappeared, too, before our divorce was final.

Out West there are no moral Shanes or Clint Eastwood characters riding into our valleys and towns to save the day by drawing their reluctant guns. There never were.

We must save ourselves.

As I see it, we must study the components of peace and emotional-spiritual strength and teach them to our children. Hippie lore.

Since Vietnam, hippie voices have been silenced by ridicule, as if the values of gentleness, peace, and love are silly and superfluous. Wars and rumors of wars abound, all fought under the absurd contradiction of "peace."

In these troubled times, our free press ignores anti-aggression demonstrations, preferring to focus instead on atrocities, fulfilling another hippie's philosophy—Jerry Mander, an advertising executive who pointed out that death "works" on television while "life" bores consumers.

Our government has been very successful at keeping us watching the uniform propaganda of television rather than reading about varied and multiple ideas and discussing them. The students I encounter in college classrooms don't even consider television consumption as a choice. It's just there.

Educators whine about needing bigger schools with more and more computers in them, with bars on the windows and police patrolling the halls. Maybe what we really need is much simpler, that is, allowing our children to follow Socrates around Athens, listening, developing the rudiments of logic and discernment.

Advertising magnates, western rednecks, and our president tell us Americans have the best lifestyle in the world, but at whose expense? And how do we know it's the best? What are we measuring it against?

Alan Watts, a 1960s Zen philosopher, said, "We have confused money with wealth," and I'll add, "In Littleton, Colorado, slaughter became confused with power."

Sex and the Single Cowboy

—Stephen Lyons

The very first time I met A. C. Riley I nearly got punched out. All I was doing was coming up behind him in my usual nonintrusive, noncompetitive, quiet, early 1970s way to introduce myself as the chief cook and bottle washer for the Colorado outfit called the Diamond Arrow Dude Ranch. A.C. was the wrangler, just in from the Lubbock Stockyards and full of all this Texas cowboy etiquette. Like don't swear in front of a guy's girlfriend; never drink less than twenty cups of black coffee a day; and, for God's sake, don't, under any circumstances, ever sneak up behind a cowpoke. You're liable to get decked.

At least that's the cowboy myth, and no one believed that crap more than A.C. Riley. In fact, he thrived on the cowboy image. A regular Marlboro Man. Whenever an attractive-looking woman stayed at the Diamond, it was always, "Yes, ma'am, no ma'am. Cowboying is lonesome, but a man's gotta do what he's gotta do." Then he'd take off his black Stetson, real gentlemanly like, while the poor woman (a Methodist just up from Houston) fell in love with him. I saw it happen a dozen times that summer.

And me just standing there fading into the background like a coatrack, hating his cowboy guts, his Texas accent, the way he held his coffee cup and cigarette with the same hand. And knowing when night came, A.C. would be rolling in the arms of that same attractive woman (by now a lapsed Methodist) with his hat on the bedpost and, if he really felt sensitive that night, he'd take his boots off. I'd once again retire alone to my tent, pet my blue heeler, Emmie, and fall asleep listening to the whirl of the Coleman lantern while reading Hermann Hesse. It was a long, lonely western summer.

In the morning, he'd start to rub it in a bit. "Did you rope your mule last night? You know you're only supposed to rope your mule if he comes up. It's bad luck to rope your mule if he doesn't come up." Why didn't I pour grease down his faded Wrangler shirt with the extra-long tails? Instead I was stuck with *Magister Ludi: The Glass Bead Game* and, yes, a summer of roping my mule whether it came up or not.

One Friday night A.C. took me to town to teach me how to pick up women. Felt sorry for me he said, living a life of celibacy in a tent, eating raisins and nuts. "I'm worried you'll go blind, Lyons." A.C. dressed me in tight Wranglers, boots, and a paisley shirt, topped with a beige hat with porcupine quills in the brim (from a roadkill). There was nothing A.C. could do about the wire-rim glasses and my liberal smirk. I must say I looked good.

At the Stockyard Bar after a few beers, A.C. poked me and said, "She's looking at you. Tip your hat to her. She's a barrel racer and you know what that means." It was difficult to assess the situation as rapidly as A.C. could, and I had no idea what sexual repertoire a barrel racer had, but for some vague reason I trusted his judgment and besides, he did this every Friday night with disgusting success and I had finished my last Hesse book, so I sauntered over as best as I could wearing Tony Lamas that were two sizes too large. Events then moved rapidly and it was to be the last time I saw A.C. that weekend. The barrel racer actually had a glass eye that wandered so it was hard to tell just who she was looking at. After we danced a couple of awkward western numbers, she ditched me for a biker. I ended up in an alley with the dry heaves.

Cowboys, bikers. What's the difference? I walked the twelve miles home to the ranch, cursing A.C. and each boot-induced blister along the way. Next day I quit the mass-cooking profession and went back to college where I studied literature. My specialty? Hermann Hesse.

A.C., last I heard, was working as a collections agent on the Navajo reservation for a shadowy car firm out of Snowflake, Arizona. A just reward if you ask me. And every Christmas for a few years I got a postcard from him with the following message: "Lyons, did you rope your mule last night? You know you're only supposed to rope your mule. . . ."

Old-Timers

—Chinle Miller

"There it is, Cleo, the Grand Canyon." I lean out over the guardrail at Desert View. "Quite a sight, isn't it?"

"You bet," my old friend Cleo smiles, blue eyes dancing in amusement, framed in weatherworn wrinkles.

The Canyon's fogged in. Cleo and I could be looking across a thirty-foot-deep arroyo, for all we can tell. It's winter, and we somehow timed our visit to coincide with an immense fog cloud. Cleo's eyes squint, trying hard to see through the dense mist tickling our eyelashes.

My friend Cleo is eighty-six years old, born in Arizona, maybe never even been out of Arizona, yet he's never seen the Grand Canyon. Cleo tells me he's not sure he believes there is such a canyon. Sure, he's seen pictures, but then they can do things with cameras—just go to any Hollywood movie, he says.

"I quit goin' to them doggone things because I couldn't read that fast," he adds, referring tongue in cheek to the days of the silent screen.

So I talk Cleo into the drive up to the Canyon by telling him that if he doesn't go now, he'll have to see it from the seat of a bus, as the Park Service is going to restrict car traffic soon. But I'm really thinking more of his age, of the cataracts that are beginning to cloud his once-clear eyes. Cleo's finally reached the status of "old-timer."

We can barely make out the rocks we're standing on—much less the immense plunge at our feet. Cleo seems to enjoy the irony as much as he would have enjoyed seeing the hypothetical Canyon.

"Kind of reminds me of the Lost Dutchman Mine," he muses. "I spent a good many years lookin' for that one. Never did have any luck."

Old-timers. Like ponderosa pine and moss rock define a landscape, the West was defined by old-timers like Cleo. Characters we fondly call them. We admire their outspoken ways, their self-sufficiency, their refusal to conform to a society that pays well for conformity. People like Cleo are our last bastions against the wave of homogeneity sweeping across our need to be unique. Our old-timers are an endangered species.

Yet the influence of Cleo's generation really wasn't what we've made it out to be. We've romanticized them, as well as their era—the fading American cowboy, the uranium prospector, the rancher, the desperado. In reality, theirs was more often a gritty, harsh existence, their tread on the land hard. In our desperation to live up to our myths, we've made their world a bigger place than it really was.

But they helped us create that sense of continuity we westerners desperately need. What will become of us when they're all gone?

It's spring, and Cleo and I are again driving up the Coconino Plateau to see the Grand Canyon, weather forecast all clear. Once more, we stop at Desert View, and Cleo gingerly steps over to the guardrail. He pauses, taking in the overwhelming display of color and depth. I can almost see him catch his breath.

"Just like them pictures, only better. I knew it would be." His blue eyes sparkle. Then he takes off his old straw Stetson. Leaning out over the Canyon, he spins the hat into the wind.

The hat rises, pauses, dips, and disappears into a background of colored sediment. I think of the millions of years it took the Canyon to mature. I think of the eighty-six years Cleo's seen and how the West has changed in that short time.

Cleo muses, "You know, my life's been a lot like that hat." He pauses, distracted by the grandeur at his feet, then adds, "I've had plenty of ups and downs, but I've always been lucky to drift around in God's country."

Shadows run along the edge of the Canyon, following sun and cloud. Far on the North Rim a cougar hunts, escorted by hopeful magpies dressed for dinner in black and white tuxedos.

Our old-timers are fading away, and with them goes a part of our beloved West. Like us, they love the desert, the sky, the wind, the forlorn coyote yip.

We'll miss them.

Remembering Ed Abbey

—Jim Stiles

Edward Abbey changed my life. He saved me from becoming a Republican. Twenty-five years after a friend of my father's handed me a worn-out copy of *Desert Solitaire* and a decade after his death, Ed Abbey is, to me, an honest hero in a time and a world where we don't allow heroes. He'd throw a beer bottle at me right now (an empty) if he were here to read these words of praise.

I still remember the first time I met him. I'd read *Desert Solitaire* a few years earlier and had abandoned my family's perverse dedication to Richard Nixon and the GOP. Now I was an Abbey groupster, one of those annoying young eco-freaks who drove a VW microbus covered with inflammatory bumper stickers. I had come west from Kentucky to live in Moab, Utah, and I had come to give Abbey a present. Carefully rolled up in a cardboard tube was a drawing of mine, a cartoon extravaganza of Glen Canyon Dam blown to smithereens.

I wanted to give my pen-and-ink doodle to my favorite author and had read on the jacket cover of *The Monkey Wrench Gang* that Abbey lived in a remote corner of the Southwest called Wolf Hole, Arizona. After long hours eyeballing road maps, I found Wolf Hole, a tiny speck on the Arizona Strip, south of St. George, Utah, and north of the Grand Canyon. So I made the long pilgrimage over rough and corrugated dirt roads to Wolf Hole.

There was nothing there. Not even a fence post. If Abbey was there, I had decided, he had concealed himself far more skillfully than I could track him. I abandoned the quest, but months later a mutual Park Service friend introduced me to Ed at a poker game in Moab, Utah, and I finally gave him the Glen Canyon Dam(n) cartoon. He was as gracious and kind as I could have hoped.

"It's Floyd Dominy Falls!" he crowed. But when I told him I'd gone all the way to Wolf Hole to give him the drawing, Abbey's grin broadened.

"Yes . . . Wolf Hole," he chuckled. "What's it like down there?"

It was the beginning of a friendship that lasted until his death in March

1989. As I got to know Abbey over the years, I only came to admire him more, in spite of, or perhaps even because of, his faults and contradictions.

Abbey reveled in confusing his adversaries and followers alike. He was contrary, but he was so damned honest about it. Once, while expounding on population control, the young feminist interviewer thought she had Ed in her crosshairs.

"But Mr. Abbey, don't you have five children of your own?"

You could see Ed's eyes grow brighter. "Yes, I do," he answered with a hint of pure joy, "but they're by five wives. That's only one per wife."

No one saw more clearly than Abbey what we as a species need to do to keep this planet of ours from sinking into a sea of sludge, but he never claimed to be the vision of perfection himself. He detested the various crowns and titles we all attempted to bestow on him.

"I'm not a guru," he often groused, "and I'm not an 'environmental leader.' I just like to throw words around."

No one threw them better. He lit fires under people. Before Abbey, writers who came to the defense of Planet Earth, like John Muir and Henry Thoreau, spoke with gentle voices. Their message was clear, but it was usually lyrical. Abbey spoke with a clenched fist and a heart full of anger: This is our land. It's all we have. It's being ripped to pieces before our very eyes. And I'm not going to just sit here and lament its passing. I'm mad. What about you?

It was that kind of passion that ignited so many of us, and I'd like to think that Abbey's life made a difference in the West. I still live in Moab and recently someone asked me how the canyon country here would be different had Abbey never lived.

On one hand, Abbey's words have helped win public acceptance of the concept of wilderness, even here in Utah. Someday, perhaps not in my lifetime, the Utah congressional delegation will introduce a decent wilderness bill.

Nearby Canyonlands National Park was once destined to become another windshield-tourist playground with paved roads and scenic loops and industrial-strength campgrounds and hotels and snack bars. But it didn't happen. Ed Abbey's hand can be seen in this.

On the other hand, I cringe when I look at Moab today, at the ever-growing assortment of fast-food restaurants and prefab motels and the hordes of adrenaline junkies who swarm over these precious rocks looking for cheap thrills. I say to myself: Not enough people have read *Desert Solitaire.*

I know Abbey would shake his head, squeeze my shoulder, and say, "Never mind all that. Our only hope is catastrophe anyway. Get out those cigars you brought and let's go for a ride."

He was so proud of that last car. It was a 1972 red Cadillac convertible. It got eight miles to the gallon.

3. Whose Public Domain?

Sharks in the Land
—*Ed Marston*

Entrepreneurs of a new breed roam the mountains and canyons of the American West these days. Like their predecessors—the timber, cattle, and mining barons—they are out to make a buck off the public domain. Yet these new land sharks don't deplore the modern notion of protecting lands as wilderness areas and parks. In fact, they embrace it.

Take Tom Chapman, a Colorado native son who, starting in the 1980s with nothing more than a real-estate broker's license, an ability to withstand unlimited public scorn, and knowledge of the land in western Colorado, has made himself wealthy. Chapman extracts millions from taxpayers by threatening to develop high-end homes on private land within national parks and wilderness areas.

He got his start in 1984 by threatening to bulldoze in roads on the north rim of Colorado's Black Canyon of the Gunnison National Monument to serve a planned subdivision—until the National Park Service paid the landowner Chapman was representing four times what it believed the land was worth.

It was a start, but his big coup came in 1993, when he used helicopters to begin to build a large cabin on private land he owned within the West Elk Wilderness in western Colorado. The Forest Service resisted Chapman until the choppers started flying. Then the agency and the Colorado congressional delegation folded. The Forest Service ginned up an appraisal showing that Chapman's 240 acres of isolated land were worth $240,000, exactly the value it put on 105 acres of Forest Service land Chapman wanted near Telluride.

Telluride residents told Gunnison National Forest Supervisor Bob Storch that the land was worth millions, but Storch, quietly backed by the Colorado delegation, pushed the trade through. After it was clear, because of sales, that the land was worth at least ten times what the Forest Service had valued it at, Storch invited me to his office so I could see that he had followed policy precisely, dotting every "i" and crossing every "t." He sincerely could not see the difference between properly completing paperwork and properly doing a job.

Neither could the Forest Service leadership. Storch, despite the enormity of his blunder, appears to be supervisor-for-life, while Forest Service staff who stick their necks out in pursuit of land protection find them chopped off.

The buying out of Chapman's West Elk holdings has allowed him to continue his assault on the public's most prized land. Today he is hard at work on protected lands around the ski towns of Crested Butte and Vail, and he is back in the Black Canyon of the Gunnison National Forest, this time selling lots.

At the moment, he has this industry largely to himself, but it won't take long for others to follow his lead. There are about 13,000 acres of wilderness inholdings in Colorado and 450,000 acres nationally. Chapman is a pioneer—a captain of industry—pointing the way toward a New West economy.

Which is not to say that he is perfect. The robber barons I most admire are frank about their opportunism. But Chapman wraps himself in the pious cloak of private-property rights. He says that wilderness and national park inholdings are incredibly valuable and that we, the federal taxpayers, are trying to rob the owners by not paying them the land's full value.

But we, the federal taxpayers, first gave the land its "full value" by creating ironclad federal land-use zoning. The foundation of Chapman's "industry" is the assumption that the wilderness or national park will always be there.

The answer is painful but obvious. When a piece of protected land is threatened by high-end development, we should immediately withdraw legislative protection or otherwise damage the surrounding public land.

When Chapman began building his log cabin in Colorado's West Elk Wilderness, a bill should have begun moving through Congress to strip the land around his cabin from wilderness status, and the Forest Service should have begun planning one of its clear-cuts. When Chapman threatened to bulldoze in roads near the Black Canyon, the National Park Service should have begun planning a dump or a trailer park for employees or visitors next to the proposed subdivision. Reasonable landowners should be bought out at reasonable prices, but threats to protected land should be met today by sacrificing the esthetic value of the surrounding public land.

Will this happen soon? No. The interior West is not now capable of defending its most valuable assets. Both the land management agencies and the congressional delegations are in shambles. The protection of these lands awaits the growth of a cadre of tough, dedicated men and women to take over from the present bureaucratic bunch and the election of congressional leaders to back them up.

In the meantime, Tom Chapman and his followers are going to prey on our public lands the way beetles prey on the region's spindly, weakened forests. It is not going to be a pretty sight.

Pay as You Play?
—*Ken Wright*

Spring: endless snow in our mountain home, an overwhelming glacier of work on my desk, and the media a nauseating blizzard of war news.

Time for a run to my personal mecca: Cedar Mesa, a big, broad, canyon-carved shelf of piñon–juniper forest in southeastern Utah, and all public land, where we are free to put our flesh back in touch with the elements and rekindle some of those primal skills of getting in and out of the back-country. This year, it's time to take our kids, now four and six, old enough for their first canyon-hiking challenge.

Imagine our surprise when we pulled up to where the two-track to a favorite canyon had once been and in its place we find a wide, bladed road with a big BLM sign instructing us to stop and please pay two dollars (eight dollars to camp overnight) for the privilege of walking around.

Pay? Yep. The Recreation Fee Demonstration Program has come to the Four Corners, as it has to more than a hundred public-land trailheads around the West.

Time to pay to play, folks, if the Forest Service, BLM, and a cartel of major recreation-equipment corporations, under the guise of the American Recreation Coalition, have their way. Begun in 1996 (cowardly, as a rider attached to an Interior appropriations bill), the Recreation Fee Demonstration Program allows public-land managers to institute fees to test the public's acceptance of the fees. Slated to end in 2004, most believe the program will be made permanent before then.

It's only fair, defenders of the program say. Why shouldn't hikers, pic-nickers, bird-watchers, hunters, fishermen, bikers, and other daydreamers pay for their use of public lands, like loggers, miners, and grazers do?

Why? Because there seems to me to be some difference between my throw-ing up a tent and wandering around the slickrock with my kids and what else I see here on my beloved Cedar Mesa: the big square scars where the BLM has chained the forest bare so grazers can try to grow forage in the desert; the below-cost Forest Service timber sale clear-cutting hundreds of acres of aspen to the north of here, on Elk Ridge; the oozy green cowpies I have to step around to read the fine print on the sign.

Fairness? No. There's a shrewder strategy behind the rec-fee demo program: What trail fees do is put those touchy-feely, nonquantifiable values of our public lands on the quantifiable economic playing field. Turn these aesthetic "uses" into paid-for amusements, and they become just more revenue-generating line items where, at last, the joy of just being outside can be compared numerically alongside all those profit-making consumptive abuses to determine the "best" uses of our public lands.

Guess which will win? Unless, of course, recreation can justify itself by generating more income, through increased fees, or developing profitable industrial tourism, or by adding revenue-generating services—but then the amusement-park cycle is on.

The problem, as I see it, is not that public lands don't pay their own way; the problem is thinking that public lands should have to pay their own way. That's the *point* of public lands: They are refuges of undeveloped, unprofitable, and unindustrialized land protected from the great cult of economics devouring big open spaces everywhere else.

To many of us, our public lands are an investment in national spiritual-health care: places held in trust so all Americans can afford to *get out*, away from our ever-more-crowded and commercialized world.

Places our kids will need even more than we do now.

Back on Cedar Mesa, I finish reading the sign and then climb back in the car. We drive on without paying, even though we risk a fine ($50 to $200). As I see it, paying the fee is a vote in favor of it. Besides, I like to be a role model for my kids. We wind and grind our way into the backcountry until we find a hidden spot above our once-hidden canyon, a great gray gash snaking away toward the San Juan River.

The kids climb out of the car and run off, cheering and doing some kind of preschool jig, shamelessly exploiting their public lands. I just watch and think: To raise kids right, we need places to raise them right.

And that is the real best use of our public lands.

Desperately Seeking Silence
—*Stephen Stuebner*

It was the first night of our spring vacation in Moab, Utah, the mountain-bike mecca of the world. On a busy weekend, our friends had snagged the last remaining campsite in the Sand Flats area, directly across from the Slickrock Trail parking lot.

My wife, Amy, and I were apprehensive about camping for the first time with our four-month-old son, Quinn. The camping area was more cramped than we liked—two parties were set up about twenty feet from our campsite on either side of us—but it seemed like it would be okay for the first night. Besides, we were exhausted from the ten-hour drive from Boise.

About 10:00 P.M., we crawled into our REI dome tent and slipped into our sleeping bags. Most of the groups around us were still awake and partying in full force. We could hear a wide assortment of rock music, but the volume seemed tolerable.

Then, 200 yards away, someone cranked up the Steve Miller Band, drowning out all of the car stereos closer to our camp. At first, the music took me down memory lane, back to May 1978 in Missoula, Montana, where I saw Steve Miller play live in the Adams Fieldhouse. The sound on this night was totally clean and crisp as it echoed off the redrock cliffs—as if Miller's electric guitar and lyrics were on stage inside our tent.

"Come on, baby, come on, baby, let's dance. . . ."

After about three songs, I heard Amy mutter a few choice expletives under her breath, and I knew this wasn't going to work. We looked at each other in the darkness and said, "Let's go get a hotel room."

Ah, camping in the great outdoors in the 1990s.

It reminded me of the first time Amy and I camped in the Slickrock area in the spring of 1987. A couple of rowdy rednecks roared through our campsite in a Ford monster truck at about 2:00 A.M. and tried to climb a vertical sandstone cliff just above our tent. They didn't make it up the wall, and we could hear the tires squeak as they tried to back down the cliff without rolling the truck. By this time, we were outside of our tent, fearing the truck might roll and crush us as it came tumbling down. I was so mad that if I had been packing my 20-gauge shotgun, I would have been tempted to open fire on the truck.

Anyone who camps in the West has similar tales of rude neighbors and sleepless nights. In many cases, people just don't know any better. No one ever taught them any backcountry manners. This is especially true for the youngest generation, which has been raised on video games, violent shoot-'em-up TV and movies, and MTV. Someone needs to teach them that the wild outback in America is a rare place where people go to get away from all of that stuff—to escape the trappings of civilization for a few precious moments and to listen to nature and gaze at the stars.

I learned these things from veteran outdoorsy folks who I camped with in the late 1970s in Montana, people who were almost militant about backcountry ethics, especially in wilderness areas. I became super-sensitive to other people's needs for space and quiet and have since bent over backward to be courteous to other folks when I meet them on the trail, regardless of whether I'm hiking with my dogs, backpacking, mountain biking, or cross-country skiing.

It's too bad that people have to be taught such seemingly obvious behaviors as being courteous to others and respecting other people's space and quiet. Yet you couldn't find a better place for newcomers to learn about outdoor ethics than Moab. It's the first contact that many new mountain bikers have to the outdoors.

The day after our late-night rock concert, following a peaceful night in the giant Super 8 motel in Moab, I decided to search for a quiet, secluded campsite farther up Sand Flats Road. It was Monday, so a number of weekenders had cleared out. I got lucky and found a perfect spot in a large alcove. As I set up camp, my spirits soared. I spent the morning in a small cave above the campsite. The only sounds were the wind blowing through the juniper trees, tiny whispers bouncing off the walls of the cave, and an occasional descending call of a canyon wren.

That night, our friends came up to our campsite for Dutch-oven chicken and apple crisp. Teri Landa was the first one to say, "Man, it's so quiet up here; it's not only a killer spot, but it's so quiet."

I turned to her and said, "That's the way it's supposed to be."

Bolting Paradise
—Steve Wolper

There's a new war these days for the West's public lands, and it doesn't involve ranchers, miners, or loggers. It centers, instead, on the giant outdoor recreation industry and its ever-growing ability to influence public policy on behalf of its customers, even at the expense of the environment.

Nearly a year ago, Undersecretary of Agriculture Jim Lyons acknowledged this new battleground when he stated that the recreation industry is poised to replace the timber industry as a major funding source for public lands.

Interestingly, it was Lyons who last month heralded the first significant display of Big Recreation's political might. At a national trade show for outdoor-equipment manufacturers in Salt Lake City, he announced that his office had overridden the chief of the U.S.D.A. Forest Service and reversed a ban on the installation of permanent bolts for climbers in federally designated wilderness areas.

The crowd—the makers and retailers of tents, boots, mountain bikes, and yes, climbing gear—heartily approved. After all, it had taken a well-orchestrated campaign to get the feds to back off. Behind the scenes, lobbyists from Recreational Equipment Incorporated (REI), the Outdoor Recreation Coalition of America (ORCA), and the Access Fund (a climbers' rights group) had bent the ears of lawmakers and administration officials, telling them that the ban would mean the end of climbing in wilderness. They might have even mentioned the potential loss of revenues makers of climbing equipment would suffer.

As a climber for thirty years, I don't argue that the wilderness bolt ban would have limited my access to many peaks and cliffs, but wilderness recreation is supposed to be engaged substantially on nature's terms and not at the expense of the resource. Drilling hundreds or thousands of holes in the rock each year to install bolts permanently alters the resource. No other user group is allowed to do this, or to leave behind physical signs of its activity without obtaining a very restrictive special-use permit.

This is the "leave no trace" wilderness ethic I thought national environmental groups embraced. However, Big Recreation also visited the offices of the nation's largest and most staunch wilderness defenders—The Wilderness Society, the Sierra Club, and the National Parks Conservation Association. And the groups gave ground, agreeing to abandon their earlier positions and oppose or at least not take a position on the bolt ban. How could they back down? The answer comes right out of the extractive industries' playbook: money and power.

REI funds a number of worthwhile projects run by conservation groups, including campaigns for the securing of new wilderness. But now the Big Recreation lobby has told the preservation organizations very plainly, but never within earshot of the press, that the recreation industry would never support any future wilderness designation if they supported the ban on fixed anchors.

Such hardball tactics will undoubtedly become a regular feature of the New West, as the recreation industry's need to sell products to public-land users overrides ecological and aesthetic concerns.

Consider the recreation lobby's appropriation of Republican Senator Slade Gorton (Washington) to the cause. In the weeks before Lyons's announcement, Gorton found himself at REI's main store in Seattle, holding a press conference with REI's CEO Wally Smith. What was the avowed antienvironmental lawmaker doing amid such a green crowd? Expressing "outrage" that climbers were being so ill-treated and announcing his proposed rider to the Interior appropriations bill that would prohibit the Forest Service from enforcing its bolt ban. This is the same Senator Gorton who is also continually "outraged" at the poor treatment our government has given to the timber, mining, and public-land grazing industries.

Gorton is the sponsor of another legislative rider backed by Big Recreation that could have an even more profound effect on wilderness. This measure would prohibit the Forest Service from managing wilderness to maintain "the subjective concept of solitude." Never mind that the Wilderness Act defines wilderness as having "outstanding opportunities for solitude or a primitive and unconfined type of recreation." Never mind that one of the most frequent complaints from visitors to wilderness is of overcrowding and a lack of "solitude." Limiting the number of visitors to wilderness is not an option Big Recreation wants the Forest Service to consider. Just think of all the backpacks, hiking boots, sleeping bags, and camp stoves that might not be sold.

It's time for the conservation community to wake up to the threat posed by the recreation industry. Today the issue is climbing bolts; tomorrow it could be a whole new definition of public lands, where, once again, the environment takes a back seat to commerce.

The Wild, at the Cellular Level

—Christina Nealson

The land above tree line is another world. Cumulus clouds snap by within reach. Sponge-moss tundra springs under my feet, as electric cerulean forget-me-nots join the thin air to ensure that I will not forget this trip.

Today I am with friends, gasping my way toward Culebra Peak in southern Colorado. Readying ourselves for the final thousand, one-step-at-a-time feet, we take a break on a rock precipice ridgeline at 13,000 feet. There's nothing like being on top of the world, vulnerable to the elements, and at peace.

Wait a minute. What's that voice? I turn to see my friend talking into his cell phone to his wife, two states away. I didn't know that he had brought the phone and am immediately torn by strong, differing opinions. On one hand, the romance of it all. I mean, what woman wouldn't love to hear her lover's voice from a mountaintop? To know that amid such beauty he is thinking of *her*? But the pit in my stomach tells me that deeper feelings prevail, feelings that have to do with the cell phone's immediate transformation of the wilderness.

"I felt the same way," said my husband several days later, "when my friend Kenny pulled out a cell phone in our hunting camp and called his girlfriend."

Yes, things are a-changing in the wild West. A study by battery manufacturer Duracell found that 38 percent of vacationers now pack a cell phone or pager. Eighteen percent bring along a personal notebook computer or electronic organizer.

I recently read about a man falling and breaking his leg while hiking in the wilderness above Boulder, Colorado. The lost hiker carried a cell phone and a handheld Global Positioning System (GPS) unit, a precision electronic navigation aid that locks into orbiting satellites and calculates exact position and movement. He called 911, gave them his precise coordinates, and was quickly rescued.

I go to wilderness to enter the cyclical time of the natural cycles and leave linear time behind. In so doing, I also leave behind the world of instant access, where phones, emails, cars, and airplanes provide fast contact with anyone in the world. It is a step from the planned, organized, domesticated world into the realm of the unexpected. Whether a meadow of mariposa lilies or a sudden lightning storm at tree line, the beautiful and dangerous surprises of wilderness keep me well-honed. I must plan carefully. I must be aware of changes in wind and weather.

A cell phone changes all of this. Suddenly, I don't have to be responsible for poor planning, silly mistakes, or bad luck. Like the hiker who broke his leg, I don't even have to take a map if I have my toys. In today's world, rescue teams with helicopters wait to save me from myself.

Colorado has approximately 3 million acres of wilderness and multitudinous millions of acres of national forest. Like its Inner Mountain West neighbors, much of its land is public. Public lands are, in fact, the partial definition of the West. For years, people have come to the forests and filled darkness with Coleman lanterns. They filled silence with music. And now they fill solitude with instant access to the technological world.

Next week, I'm riding my horse into the wilderness to camp alone for a few days. I'll pack a .357 on my hip. Three shots, three whistles, three of any noise is a distress signal. This is closer to the West I came to live in twenty years ago. A place where danger and beauty coincide, where I am part of the food chain, vulnerable to weather changes, dependent upon instinct. A place where personal responsibility gets the utmost test.

In today's sanitized world, we've minimized risk so much that the psyche deadens and violence becomes more and more perverse. There's a reason why cultures ritualize violence. The psyche and soul need tests. This is why rodeo still lives in the West. Why cowboys still brave the elements with their stock across miles of dangerous terrain, and why people leave the safety of their homes with a pack on their back and head into the mountains.

Phones and computers change the wilderness as much as forbidden roads and chain saws. Perhaps more.

When River Guiding Was Grand
—*Brad Dimock*

I began my "career" as a Grand Canyon river guide in 1971, in the heart of what we later referred to as the clueless years. Few boatmen had more than a couple dozen trips under their belt; some were on their first. We had few wizened veteran guides to tell us where to hike, how to get through Hance Rapid at low water, or how best to manage a disgruntled guest. We were on our own, figuring it out as we went along. A trip that finished at the right place, on the right day, was a good one.

These were expeditions in a true sense of the word. We were learning tricks and techniques daily, making progress—and truly magnificent blunders. Motor rigs ripped stem to stern, or beached a hundred yards from the river after the river level fell. These were expeditions, all right, for passengers paying less than fifty dollars a day. We all struggled together.

What made it work—the thing that was so profoundly different then—was that we were trusted. Not just by the passengers, our bosses, and the National Park Service, but by society as a whole. We were given a boat and a group of passengers at the launch ramp, expected to do our best and show up at the other end. How we did it was left to our wits, judgment, and discretion. Just bring 'em back happy.

The learning curve remained steep for several years. We learned how to get the boats through with a degree of predictability. We began preparing meals that were more than just edible. We learned about geology and the ecosystem and found ways to convey it intelligibly. By the mid-eighties, Grand Canyon had a self-taught cadre of highly trained professionals running top-quality adventures.

Somewhere toward the end of the 1980s, it all began to sour. Although we were performing at ever-higher levels of professionalism and training, the trust we thrived on disappeared, bit by bit.

I struggled for years to find someone, something, to blame. Was it the outfitting companies? The insurance companies? The Park Service? It wasn't really any of them. It was a societal shift, bulldozing its way through the culture, until even down in the Big Ditch, where we'd thought we were immune, we found ourselves inundated. The ballooning affluence of the Reagan–Bush years finally caught up with us.

As the financial stratification of the culture progressed, our clientele grew wealthier. Schoolteachers, nurses, farmers, and just plain folks were priced out, to be replaced with doctors, lawyers, and the Silicon Valley nouveau-riche.

Trip marketing began gearing toward the Outdoor Material Culture, the yup-scale deluxe cruise, the predictable and comfortable "wilderness experience." As expectations mutated, complaints became more numerous, yet more trivial. Clients wanted "service."

Meanwhile, the ever-growing private boating population was locked into a small, archaic allocation system, and it clamored for a bigger share of the pie. At the same time, the Park Service began looking seriously at its mandate to manage Grand Canyon for wilderness values.

Outfitters, no longer owning stake-bed trucks full of war-surplus rafts but million-dollar businesses, became nervous and listened to the whisperings of lawyers and insurance agents. They formed powerful trade organizations—America Outdoors and Grand Canyon River Outfitters Association—complete with lobbyists and political contributions.

Down on the Colorado River, the "resource," running at or beyond capacity for more than a decade, began to suffer visibly. More beaches and trails had to be rebuilt, reinforced, artificially stabilized—steps constructed, banks rip-rapped with driftwood logs, trails marked ever more grossly and unmistakably to mitigate trampling.

The river guide was eyed with ever more scrutiny. A profession that was once defined by its sheer lack of definition became quantified, qualified, measured. We had somehow come to be on trial.

For me, the final straw came last year, when boatmen were legally presumed to be drug users. Unless we could prove otherwise through urine testing, we could no longer work in Grand Canyon. We became guilty until proven innocent.

Perhaps it was inevitable. The Grand Canyon river experience is one of the more magical treasures on a planet that has far, far too many people. In a culture that reveres material wealth above all else, bottom-line economics and paranoiac policy making are as natural an outgrowth as the desperate need to escape from the same. Grand Canyon is caught, viselike, in the middle. Drug testing was just the dying canary.

Grand Canyon is still a wonderful place. River trips are still changing people's lives. But the trends are sinister. And unless we change direction, as the old Chinese proverb states, we will almost assuredly end up where we are headed.

Cult of the Lazy Hunters
—*Cody Beers*

The average elk hunter in Wyoming can't kill an elk. I'm convinced of it. And I'm saddened and sickened by it. Scared, too.

I'm a hunter in my spare time. As an employee of the Wyoming Game and Fish Department, I'm paid to defend hunting, but I no longer can defend the things hunters are doing to my state's public lands and wildlife. They're messing up my hunting, and future hunting opportunities for my sons.

Armed with all-terrain vehicles or four-wheel-drive pickups, a disregard for signs, and few to no ethics or personal pride, some of them are leaving tracks in places where they have no business. These places were once roadless areas where elk and other species could be found with a little effort. Now they are areas of rundown habitat and scarce wildlife. This irresponsible behavior is happening in wilderness areas, on U.S.D.A. Forest Service lands, Bureau of Land Management lands, state lands, and Wyoming Game and Fish Department's wildlife habitat management areas.

This past fall Wyoming hunters pioneered more than forty new four-wheel-drive roads within the Wick Wildlife Habitat Management Area near Arlington. They drove around road-closed signs and paid no attention to the Game and Fish's white-arrow travel management program. In the Cow Creek Mountain public access area, hunters turned a block of public land into a maze of ATV trails from one end of the area to the other. It's little wonder that I didn't find any elk there this fall.

A number of reasons have been offered to explain the proliferation of ATV use and abuse of four-wheel-drive pickups: ATVs are easy to get, and their sale is fueled by those pushy advertisers who capitalize on some people's "need" to randomly drive off roads. Slick campaigns trumpet the advantages of ATVs for America's aging baby-boomer population, which wants easier ways to access the playgrounds of their youth.

I discount all these excuses. Bottom line: The majority of hunters are lazy.

I guess I shouldn't be surprised. Society at the end of the twentieth century craves whatever is easy. Fast-food restaurants are found on every corner, sandwiched between the local quick lube or video rental/convenience store. Hunters are not immune to this trend. Look inside the cover of a Cabela's catalog. You can buy two-way radios, night-vision binoculars, laser sights, ATV winches. The ridiculous list goes on. The marketing pitch is aimed toward lazy hunters who are willing to pay whatever it takes to improve their so-called chances of success.

I know not everyone agrees with me, including some friends. Driving off roads on public land, they maintain, is their God-given constitutional right as Americans. Baloney. Off-road use wasn't a thought when the Bill of Rights was penned. Your rights stop where public land begins.

Many ATV users maintain that they park their machines when they reach their hunting areas. Wrong, again. I've never seen a parked ATV while I've been hunting. What I have seen are so-called hunters clearing paths through the timber with a chain saw so they can drive to their downed game. Anybody crazy enough to attempt that should have their vehicle and chain saw confiscated, hunting privileges revoked, and mandatory jail time.

When I hunted elk five days this fall, I walked. Two of us used pack frames to haul our elk quarters a mile off a mountain to our parked pick-up truck. Another member of our group was fortunate enough to harvest his cow elk near an old two-track road on a private ranch where we had permission to be. But it took eight long days of foot hunting before he gained access to the ranch.

Call it sweat equity. Gimmicks and cool gadgets weren't required. Hard work and dedication were. We played within the rules.

It's time to use peer pressure to end abuse of our public lands. If you see someone breaking the rules in the field, tell him (or her). Attend public meetings and demand stiffer penalties and stricter enforcement from Forest Service and BLM officials.

If you're mad, but you're also a lazy, slob hunter who abuses your privileges, too bad. I doubt whether you're still reading. If you are, get off your lazy butt this winter, join a health club, take a walk, get in shape, breathe in some fresh air, and be a hunter.

Freedom Is Just Another Word for Snowmobiles
—John Adams

It was fortunate that I could ski faster than my friend Mark Tokarski, because, like a 200-pound mosquito in a red stocking cap, he was pursuing me, belting out this incredibly annoying whining sound: "YEEEEENNNNGGGHHHH." Foolishly, as we shushed along cross-country trails on the Bitterroot Divide, I had commented what a rare pleasure it was to hear the sound of snow plop from overladen pine branches, rather than the whine of snowmobiles.

"Do you want me to make that noise, so you feel at home?" Tokarski asked and, without waiting for a reply, launched into his impression of a snowmobile engine. I rewarded him at the top of the pass with a well-packed snowball.

Regrettably, real snow machines are not so easily dealt with. Advocates claim snowmobile use in Montana went up 73 percent in the last decade, and U.S. sales doubled between 1992 and 1996. Powerful new machines, no longer prone to sinking in deep powder, go virtually anywhere there is snow cover—even areas that are officially closed to snowmobiles. YEEN-NGGHH.

Snow machines are not entirely a bad thing, I sometimes reflect. I wholeheartedly support recreational use of our public lands, and folks ought to enjoy the great outdoors in winter. As the International Snowmobile Industry Association once commented, "The sport of snowmobiling has acted . . . to greatly mollify [sic] the sedentary nature of winter activities."

I'm sensitive to the charge that environmentalists want to lock up the West and make it into some kind of huge, empty preserve where, clad in polar fleece, we can freely seek hot springs, quaint cappuccino shops, and a mate with the right kind of trust fund. Still, I believe we could do worse to the West; we could turn it into a 50-million-acre amusement park with a Wall Drug in every town, jetboats on every river, and snowmobiles on every mountain.

For a glimpse of this nightmare, take Wallace, Idaho. At first glance, it looks like just another small town on Interstate 90, but it is much more, or much less, depending on your perspective. The town's boosters tout Wallace as "the world's largest snowmobile destination," featuring 1,000 miles of ATV trails. Silver Country Inc., a local public relations firm, describes the area as "the Waikiki of the 21st century . . . a recreation preserve . . . the world's largest Eco-Disneyland."

"Picture yourself going back to a time straight out of a Clint Eastwood western," the company says in one brochure. "Where horses were tied up in front of the saloon, now parking is reserved for Arctic Cats, Yamahas and Ski Doos. . . . From Lookout Pass you can open up the throttle on a 55-mile loop deep into the Montana wilds, and right up to the front of Old West casinos."

Freedom, Wallace suggests, is making your own rules and conquering the backcountry without ever getting off your butt. Driving a machine through America's last wildlands is a shorthand claim to outdoor skills, self-reliance, and other frontier virtues. Instead of spending a lifetime in the woods, now all it takes to become Jim Bridger is the money to rent a Yamaha Wolverine four-by-four.

New technology is allowing snowmobiles and ATVs to invade territory they couldn't get to in the past. Sales are also up. Trail-legal ATVs that go sixty miles per hour now outsell street motorcycles, and snowmobile sales are soaring.

If the ORV/theme park experience were simply one choice of many available in the West, its rise would be less disturbing. Unlike hikers, hunters, equestrians, and others who prefer "quiet trails," however, ORVs do not complement existing use; they replace it. In a 1994 University of Montana survey, 91 percent of trail hikers said walking is incompatible with motorcycles, and three-quarters of cross-country skiers couldn't stomach the presence of snowmobiles.

Yet the state of Montana spends nearly $1 million a year promoting ATV and snowmobile use, and an astonishing 58 percent of national forest trails in Montana are open to some type of motorized vehicle.

If we are acting out our national myths astride snowmobiles, if we accept that driving an incredibly pollutive machine through the last wildlands of the Lower 48 is "freedom," then we are dooming ourselves and our children to a future as consumptive, insubstantial, and debilitatingly mindless as those very rides.

In the same way that sharing a family meal is more rewarding than eating a TV dinner, real engagement with nature yields unexpected benefits. Hiking and skiing the Bitterroots, one may learn—over time—patience and strength, caution and confidence, and the satisfaction of accomplishing difficult physical tasks. One has the opportunity to surprise a bear, smell the vanilla odor of Ponderosa bark, learn how to handle a canoe or quarter an elk.

These rewards are neither instant nor guaranteed, but they have been an invaluable part of human experience from time immemorial. We are fools to throw them away for a blaze of adrenaline and a haze of blue smoke.

Happy Campers
—Lou Bendrick

Every summer, my husband and I head for the woods, flushed with optimism and giddy with anticipation. The maps are crisp, the Coleman fuel cans are full, and the road is open.

Every summer, I forget that the reality of camping is different from that pictured in Dodge Dakota commercials and my mind.

I imagine vigorous, seamless hikes. In truth, my walks entail a ream of moleskin, a wheel of duct tape, numerous applications of sunblock, the removal of several layers of high-tech clothing quickly followed by reapplication of clothing, incessant adjustments to pack, boots, shoelaces, and attitude, five to ten pee breaks (due to zealous obeisance to the "copious and clear" rule), two to fifteen Kodak moments, and several instances of feigning interest in wildflowers when I am really just catching my breath.

My husband has his own ways of fiddling. He's a cartophile extraordinaire. He doesn't just like maps, he loves them. Camping starts with the *Rand McNally Road Atlas*, which he has highlighted. His backpack holds a library of road maps, folded like origami. (I remember the first time I refolded one of his maps wrong. He looked as shocked and horrified as someone who was watching his house burn.) At every trail junction, he spreads the maps out like a mad general, smooths his hands over them, then points and says, "Look! We're right here."

Far from an honest and simple experience, camping in tandem is based on complex and well-calculated lies. Consider the following common camp statements:

"Really, you have the last Mint Milano."

"I'm really not that cold. I just need some calories."

"I've never been to this area with another woman/man."

"We're almost there."

"Just a quarter mile now."

"Your hair is not so bad."

"You don't smell too bad."

"My back feels better when I sleep on the ground."

"Mocha Powerbars are pretty good."

"As long as you don't surprise 'em, yer fine."

Every year, too, I fall victim to the fantasy that I will meet nature on its own terms. I hope I will be blessed to hear the bugle of an elk or catch a glimpse of an eagle. In most cases, my encounters with nature, "red in tooth and claw," involve fat campsite animals.

These creatures, tame and ruined by the flotsam and jetsam of campers, include corpulent, aggressive marmots; cue ball–shaped whiskyjacks and obese squirrels that appear with the first crinkle of a dehydrated meal bag.

The hearty, nourishing meals I had envisioned (venison stew with spring vegetables baked in a Dutch oven) are, in reality, low-brow: Tuna Helper followed by two packets of blisteringly hot cocoa served in an insulated cup that still tastes like Lipton's tomato soup. After two days of packet meals, I start to indulge in incessant food fantasies.

"When I get back, I'm having mashed potatoes and brownies," I'll say, while swigging out of a Nalgene bottle wrapped with duct tape.

My husband will try to trump me. "I'm having surf and turf with a baked potato with sour cream and fresh chives," he'll say, cutting a bruised apple with a dirty Swiss Army knife.

We continue this culinary masochism until we are resentful of our couscous and gorp. Depressed, we usually switch topics and begin picking on philistine RV-ers who happen to be eating a lot better than we are.

On the last day of camping, one of us inevitably spills fuel in the back of the Subaru or rubs Dr. Bronner's peppermint soap into an eyeball.

Nevertheless, last year I slipped out of my sticky down bag at 3:00 A.M. to answer nature's least romantic call. I had forgotten my head lamp, so I slammed into the campsite picnic table. I sat down to massage the throbbing knee and looked up. Above me was the Milky Way as I had not seen it in years. An owl hoo-hooed somewhere in the blackness.

In the morning I wrapped my cold, pink fingers around a cup of coffee as the sun came up. Camp coffee is always better than I remember.

Wilderness Is No Handicap
—*Paul Larmer*

I finally learned how to ski this winter. It took the prodding of a friend and the skills of an instructor who specializes in helping people with disabilities, but now, at thirty-seven, I have experienced the joy of swishing down a dazzling white slope in the Rocky Mountains.

I needed the special instructor because I have only one functioning leg. Like every other sport I have tried, skiing took some adjustments. My instructor showed me how to use modified crutch skis, dispensed timely hints as I clumsily fell a dozen or so times in a very flat practice bowl; and then set me loose on the bunny hill.

What a blast.

Gliding down the gentle hill, I could hardly imagine the adrenaline rush people experience on the expert runs high above. Some one-legged skiers and sled-skiers rise to that challenge, but I felt just fine where I was. I've learned over the years that you do what fits, and you don't hold a grudge against those who can do more.

I've come to think about wilderness in the same way.

Recently I attended a conference in Salt Lake City sponsored by the Western States Coalition, a group of conservative western legislators who have pooled their resources to better fight off environmentalists and federal land managers, whom they see as the biggest threat to the "western way of life."

One speaker got up and spoke disparagingly of the "elitist environmentalists" who were pushing for legislation to protect more than five million acres of roadless wilderness in Utah. "They want to lock it all up as a playground for the young and healthy," he said. "Most people, including our old people and the disabled, won't be able to hike into that beautiful country. Is that fair?"

Good question.

I have felt the frustration of not being able to do the things others do easily. In high school I watched my two able-bodied brothers star on the basketball team. I could sink nine out of ten free throws and hold my own in a game of H-O-R-S-E, but I had to accept that I would never be a player on the team.

I remember my angry embarrassment as a kid when, after waiting an hour in line, I was told I couldn't ride Space Mountain at Disney World because there was no place to put my crutches. Last year, I took my children to Disney World and was happily surprised to see that all rides are now accessible to people with all kinds of disability. Activists have accomplished much over two decades.

Still, the question pulls on me: Is wilderness unfair to people who will never be able to visit it? Though I respect the idea of equal access to public resources, the answer is "No!"

The people who created the Wilderness Preservation System more than thirty years ago weren't elitist or prejudiced. They recognized that wilderness is about more than equal recreational opportunity. It's about clean waters, habitat for wildlife, and keeping some vestige of the wild to feed our hungry souls.

I feel used when people with an agenda categorize people like me as victims. I should have told that man at the conference "If you think that every last acre of public land should be roaded and developed, fine. That's at least an honest—if misguided—opinion. Just don't hold me up as your shield."

As it is, I have plenty of access to public lands. The national forests alone have more than 400,000 miles of road carved through them. National parks have wide, paved roads and trails and handicap camp sites within easy rolling distance of restrooms.

I am glad long-closed doors have been opened to the disabled. My parents made sure I could play Little League baseball. The coaches bent the rules so that I could bat and have a teammate run the bases for me. I was a decent pitcher, but I knew when my last game ended at age thirteen that my competitive hurling days were over. High school ball was like the big leagues, and I couldn't imagine pushing to play under a set of rules different from everyone else's.

Wilderness has its own rules, too. High in the mountains or in the desert, the weather can turn in an instant, and a hillside can give way before you even take a step. Everyone who enters takes a risk, and that's how it should be. No four-wheelers or snowmobiles to make the experience easier and safer. It's the big leagues.

I will never take a week-long solo hike into the Sawtooths of Idaho, the Maroon Bells of Colorado or the Aldo Leopold Wilderness in New Mexico, but I revel in their existence. It's okay that I can't go everywhere and do everything.

Still, I can't wait to hit the ski slopes again. Sitting here, the possibilities seem almost limitless. Maybe I'll try that black diamond run yet.

Grazing: The Hard Facts
—*Susan Zakin*

The drunk who said it was right. Denial is not a river in Egypt. But it may be a river in New Mexico. Or Arizona. Or Nevada or Utah. Maybe Montana. The river is twenty feet wider than it was, say, in 1840. The only cottonwood on its banks is just about that old, magnificent but half dead. Trout don't swim in the water. Cowbirds, not flycatchers, nest on the banks.

That's the picture drawn by a comprehensive scientific paper published in the most recent *Journal of Soil and Water Conservation*. Range scientist Joy Belsky spent six years rounding up 143 government reports and peer-reviewed scientific research on livestock grazing along streams and rivers in the West. Her report, "Survey of Livestock Influences on Stream and Riparian Ecosystems in the Western United States," shows that the jury is not out on the environmental effects of grazing. It's bad. Period.

Belsky and a number of her colleagues, including Robert Ohmart of Arizona State University, now predict that if livestock grazing in the West isn't severely cut back, restoration will become impossible. They estimate that this will happen within thirty to fifty years.

Consider the facts: Already, 80 percent of the streams and riparian ecosystems in arid regions of the western United States have been damaged by livestock grazing. That's from the U.S. Department of Interior, circa 1994. This damage isn't just from way back in frontier days. A 1990 U.S. Environmental Protection Agency report on grazing based on extensive field observations in the late 1980s revealed that riparian areas throughout much of the West are in "their worst condition in history."

Although Belsky works for a conservation group, the tiny, Portland-based Oregon Natural Desert Association, she said she made an extra effort to seek out papers that would buttress claims by grazing supporters. These include the idea that the hooves of a 1,000-pound animal act like rototillers, helping promote plant growth by churning up soil. *Au contraire*, said Belsky.

"We looked very hard for papers that showed benefits and couldn't find any," Belsky said. "There were papers that showed no effects. Usually the authors themselves pointed out that something had gone wrong, either with the research methodology or an unusual event, like a flood. Every paper that cited a positive or neutral effect, we cited."

Given this data, it's easy to understand why the overwhelming majority of western salmon and trout are threatened or endangered and why native and neotropical migratory birds are losing ground almost as fast. Yet Belsky's paper also cites statistics indicating that the number of cattle in the West has more than doubled since 1940.

Telling people that the cowboy has no chaps is less popular than ever. Luckily, Belsky, a native Texan, is bulletproof. As one of the pioneering women in her field, she has always needed to be twice as rigorous as her male counterparts. She's also better trained than many of them, with a master's degree from the Yale University School of Forestry and a Ph.D. from the University of Washington. Her decade of research into grasslands ecology in East Africa received consistent National Science Foundation funding.

Voices like Belsky's are usually drowned out by national environmental groups focused on land acquisition, like the Sonoran Institute and The Nature Conservancy. These groups are propping up ranching in the West, gambling that they can rein in the worst grazing practices. Privately, their staffers have told me they're well aware of the destructive effects of grazing, but that's not what they tell ranchers or even news reporters. If you read reports issued by these groups or articles in *The New York Times* or most of the big eastern papers in which they're quoted, you'd think that a cattle ranch is really just a big, beautiful park.

The dirty truth is that most of these groups have been acting like realestate wheeler-dealers for so long, their people are starting to think that way. All that land just gets them salivating. So they're not being straight with the American public about the risks involved.

Who's the David and who's the Goliath? Sometimes it's confusing out here in the New West. Just like in Washington, D.C., the best sound bite wins. That's not Belsky's lookout. She's not going to ramble on about the cowboy myth, even though she grew up in Abilene, Texas.

"Oh, years ago that was all stripped from me, adjectives and things," she laughs. "I'm a scientist. This is as popular as I'm going to get."

This doesn't sound hopeful, but who knows? A good old girl from Abilene is probably the only one with the, er, prairie oysters, to take on the good old boys.

My Grandpa, the Eco-Rancher

—Mervin Mecklenberg

I was having coffee, recently, with an ecology-minded friend I respect. She began telling me how bad grazing is for grasslands, and I nodded and acted as if I were listening. I was really thinking about my grandfather, who once made his living by grazing cattle.

The last time I saw my grandfather, I had yet to hear the word "riparian." As far as I knew, grazing was not considered a bad thing by environmental groups, and ranchers, although they were suspicious of the movement, could still say "environmentalist" without an accompanying four-letter adjective.

Since then the range war has heated up in the West. Environmental groups have begun promoting prairie dogs and mountain plovers as the grasslands' equivalents of the spotted owl, and ranchers are starting to worry that the list of endangered species might soon include them.

I might have become a rancher like my grandfather, but I showed too little enthusiasm. I was young and didn't understand the possibilities, so instead I went to school and eventually found a job working at a newspaper.

When I was very young, all I wanted was to be like my grandfather. We called him Pappa, and he had a certain way of wearing his hat, a certain way of looking at a person as if he could tell not only whether your shoes were tied and your nose was running but what you were thinking. No matter what was happening, he was in control. There was no situation he could not handle, or so I thought.

At the end of his life, this was taken from him. I had heard he was ill— a stroke—and although this bothered me greatly, I was busy in college. What a stroke could mean to a person like my grandfather hadn't sunk in. Then the phone rang, and I learned that Pappa was in a hospital just two blocks from my campus.

It was good I already knew the man in the bed was Pappa; otherwise, I would not have recognized him. Half of his face was limp, and in place of the quick, insightful eyes, there was a pained, lost, helpless expression.

Although I was afraid to admit it, he was dying. I reserved an hour every day to sit by his bed. Sometimes he knew I was there, sometimes he didn't.

There were instances, rare but very important to me, when the old will solidified in his eyes, and he sat up like his own self. At these times he talked to me, often about his ranch. He emphasized how hard he worked to protect a particularly fragile piece of land, resisting a temptation through economic hard times that would have been too much for a lesser person: "For twenty years I kept the cows off that land. For twenty years."

These were, perhaps, the last intelligent words he spoke to me—statements about ecology that were more than merely impassioned. They were fierce. It was not a kind of environmentalism that a person learns in school. This was a caring for the land that was born out of an intimate relationship with it, a relationship that is connected to the well-being of the rancher and his family.

When I remember Pappa, I see him stepping out of his pickup onto the range grass, the felt cowboy hat he always wore shading his face. I see him stooping down, checking the small plants like a gardener, making sure they would be there next year as well as this. The health of the grass was, for him, a matter of survival. Without it, there would be no cows, no ranch, and his family would be scattered.

Because ranching is big news in my part of the West, I have talked to many ranchers. I have drunk coffee with them at their kitchen tables and eaten lunches and dinners with their families. I have ridden around in pickups with them and looked at their cows and discussed their ranching operations. I have been impressed at how much in common many of them have with my grandfather—not only in demeanor but in attitude toward the land.

Not all ranchers are good ranchers, but those who practice their trade well know their grasslands in a way that is not possible for most of us. Like my grandfather, they tend to be ecology minded because ecology, for them, is a matter of survival.

I believe my ecologist friend would have liked my grandfather. Some things he had to say she might dislike, and I'm certain that if she mentioned prairie dogs in glowing terms, he would become angry. But if they talked until they got down to what really matters—the land and their feelings toward it—they would discover they weren't that far apart.

Up in Arms Over Idaho

—*Stephen Stuebner*

In early June 1996, Mark Lisk, Todd Walker, and I took an early-morning walk to the top of the Bruneau River canyon, a little-known scenic jewel in southwest Idaho. It was about 6 A.M.

Lisk, a professional photographer, was hoping to capture a brilliant morning light show at the edge of the 500-foot-deep red-rock chasm. As dawn broke, tiny wisps of clouds turned lipstick-pink against the backdrop of a pale-blue sky. Lisk had his light show.

And then, an F-15 from Mountain Home Air Force Base flew over us, several thousand feet above. I saw the jet glide silently across the sky with a white plume tailing behind, and I knew, from previous experience, that in seconds we would hear the delayed effect of a thunderous noise following in its wake.

Booooommmmm! The silence of an otherwise poetic moment shattered.

Lisk immediately cursed the F-15. Walker, a relatively quiet and thoughtful guy, didn't say anything at first. As we walked back to camp, we debated the Air Force's proposed expansion of training exercises over the top of the Owyhee Plateau.

The Air Force has had a 110,000-acre dummy bomb range south of the air base since World War II. In four attempts since the late 1980s, the Air Force has tried to create an air-to-ground training range encompassing several million acres over the top of several candidate wilderness areas, wild and scenic rivers, and the Duck Valley Indian Reservation.

Walker, a native of Colorado, has been an active outdoorsman his entire life. Despite his low-key demeanor, he's a Class 5 daredevil rafter. He said, "You know, I like seeing Air Force jets flying over the Bruneau canyon. These guys have to train to provide for our national defense, and to me, it looks pretty cool. I bet it'd be a blast to fly in one of those jets."

Mark and I were surprised by his response. "Oh really," we said. "Huh."

As an Idaho journalist, I've covered all four of the Air Force's proposals to enhance combat readiness in the Owyhees. It's difficult to argue with their contention that the old postage-stamp range doesn't make sense in the

1990s. But if you look outside the box of the Mountain Home AFB proposal, you see three of the nation's best tactical training ranges a half-hour flight away in Utah and Nevada: the Utah Test and Training Range, over two million acres; Nellis Air Force Range, the single largest training range in the United States at over three million acres; and the Navy's bombing range at Fallon, Nevada, another two million acres.

Cast a wider view of the West, and you find extensive training ranges for all branches of the military in California, New Mexico, Arizona, and Alaska. Now that it lacks sufficient enemies around the world, the Defense Department wants to play more war games over the top of American soil.

I'll be the first to admit that I lack the perspective of a war veteran. I graduated from high school in 1976, one year after the end of the Vietnam War. I grew up in a Republican household in which my father preached how we must stem the tide of Communism and nuke the evil Soviet empire.

At the University of Montana, I took courses on U.S. foreign relations and gained a broader perspective. I learned that the U.S. military had badly misinformed its citizens about what was really happening in Vietnam, and that, by the time President Johnson knew what was up, we were in so deep we couldn't get out. I learned about the military-industrial complex and intra-service rivalry.

The military-industrial complex is still out of control. No one, not President Bush, not President Clinton, has had the political guts to intervene. Our faithful members of Congress are so captive to the political big-money game of bringing home the pork—that is, protecting home military bases and construction projects—that Americans have yet to receive a much-deserved peace dividend.

According to the General Accounting Office, in 1996 the Defense Appropriations Committee spent $10.4 billion on weapons programs not requested by the Pentagon! We spend $265 billion a year on defense, the largest single expenditure outside of Social Security. Absent competition from the Soviet Union, U.S. defense contractors are now the leaders in weapons exports, racking up $100 billion in foreign arms sales since 1990.

We are now in a global arms race with ourselves.

Americans should demand accountability with respect to our military, both in terms of weapons programs and spending. Maybe more training areas are needed. But up to this point, no one has forced the Department of Defense to show us the grand plan.

I think I know why. They don't want us to know.

The Smell of a Forest Healing
—*Rocky Barker*

The skies of Boise are filled with smoke today, a sight and smell that rekindle a momentary twinge of fear.

The U.S.D.A. Forest Service is intentionally burning thousands of acres of the Boise National Forest this spring. The agency hopes that by setting small fires under controlled conditions it can prevent a conflagration that would burn down hundreds of thousands of acres and turn the forest to brush.

Safe in my backyard near the Boise River I have nothing to fear except the possibility that the smoke will make my sinuses throb, but the odor takes me back to 5:00 A.M., September 7, 1988, when the Yellowstone fires nearly caught me near Old Faithful.

I had spent a month following the fires around the park, sleeping in my car, and eating in fire camps. I witnessed some of the largest firestorms seen in this century. It made me a little arrogant and just plain stupid. On that September afternoon I was watching a 200-foot-high wall of flames from only yards away—without supervision.

Suddenly the wind changed and the fire began sucking all of the oxygen from the stand of lodgepole pine where I stood. The sky turned black as night. With fist-sized embers flying past my head, I ran the fastest 100-yard dash my legs could muster to the safety of a parking lot.

When I turned around, the forest where I had stood lit up like gasoline to a match. I was never more scared in my life.

The fires that burn this spring on the Boise and across the West are the legacy of the great debate that started that seminal season in American fire history. Scientists knew before 1988 that fire was a part of the natural rhythm of forests, but only a few recognized how fundamental fire was to the ecological health of forests. Foresters, steeped in the traditional view that they could grow a forest better than nature, still saw fires mostly as a threat.

Yellowstone's fires, more than any other single event, changed their world. Now federal agencies—led by many of the same men and women who retreated across Yellowstone that summer—plan to set as many as 3 million acres ablaze this year.

A major debate remains over the national fire policy and forest management, but the lines of the debate have clearly changed.

I remember the Forest Service supervisor who in 1988 was quick to blame the Park Service's natural fire policy. He bragged to me that his own bulldozer-cut firebreaks and expansive clear-cuts would stop any fire. The very next day the wind shifted to the east, carrying the fire across three bulldozer breaks and through clear-cuts so huge they could be seen from space.

Few forest firefighters would make such a claim today—after the last decade in which giant firestorms swept through Boise National Forest, Oakland and Malibu, California, and Colorado's Storm King Mountain where fourteen firefighters died in 1994.

Within Boise National Forest, managers are trying to mend a forest much different from the one that existed before the settling of the West. Then ponderosa pine forests grew tall and wide in open, parklike stands. Fire naturally burned through these relatively dry areas in intervals from ten to thirty years, clearing away all the younger trees and bushes before they could establish themselves. The tall pines would survive because of their thick, fire-resistant orange bark.

When modern man entered the picture a century ago this natural balance was upset. The small, frequent fires that had cleared away the undergrowth were now fought with increasing efficiency. Loggers came in and harvested the larger, more desirable ponderosa pines, leaving the white fir and Douglas fir.

That left the forest ripe for giant fires. Beginning in 1989, a wave of huge fires started that has left hundreds of thousands of acres blackened.

Before 1986 fires burned an average of 3,000 acres annually. Since then 63,000 acres—a twenty-one-fold increase—have burned annually.

Foresters now want to burn 30,000 acres of forest a year in the spring until they restore the forest to its previous state and then let nature once again take its course. Similar programs have been proposed throughout the West by Interior Secretary Bruce Babbitt. That means thousands of us who choose to live in western cities like Boise for the high quality of life now have to periodically breathe pollution more at home in Los Angeles.

And that's the rub. Foresters may recognize the positive effects of fire, but the public remains skeptical. Add the smoke, and an aggressive burning policy may be as hard to sustain as the illusion of our control over the forces of nature.

As for me, once I get past the fear, I don't mind the tangy smoke. It's the smell of a forest healing.

4. Political Turmoil

Lost in God's Country

—*Stephen Lyons*

In Post Falls, the school board considers adopting a creationism curriculum.

In Coeur d'Alene, Aryan Nation leader Richard "I Hate You" Butler and his merry band of racists make plans for a "One Hundred Man March" through the city, while the mayor wrings his hands.

Kootenai County commissioners declare the county an English-only territory, then wonder why its citizens object. Commissioner Ron Rankin says those who object are "a non-entity, a paranoid clack."

The same commission says that too much is made of Martin Luther King Jr. Day.

In Oldtown, a Bonner County councilman puts up an Idaho Militia sign along Highway 41. The same county's commissioners abolished the planning department.

Mississippi in the 1950s? A bad novel about Louisiana? No, business as usual in Idaho at the Millennium.

You might think I'm too harsh on the Gem State. After all, Idaho is a leader. It leads the nation in child abuse incidents and deaths, and if not for South Dakota, it would lead the nation in the least amount of money spent per capita for child welfare in 1996 (seventeen dollars). Idaho is a leader in not immunizing its children against whooping cough, an ailment that should have gone the way of polio.

In its evaluation of state welfare policies, Tufts University's Center on Hunger and Poverty recently ranked Idaho dead last. Idaho received a score of minus 15.5 out of a possible score of 22. The message is clear: Don't try to live here if you are poor.

Idaho also leads in the highest number of dumb statements by its congressional delegation, led by Representative Helen Chenoweth, who said last year that Hispanics and African-Americans were not interested in moving to northern Idaho because "The warm-climate community just hasn't found the colder climate that attractive." Colder, indeed.

For fifteen years I've pondered why Idaho lags behind the country in innovation and diversity. Why 60 percent of its fourth graders read at a third-grade level or lower. Why the state's governmental leaders don't make life so unbearable for the Aryan Nations, Bo Gritz, and the militia that they choose to live somewhere else—like Mars. Why Randy Weaver was canonized in Idaho for using his family as a body shield. Why business leaders don't tell us the truth about lost income and jobs due to the state's national image as a haven for racists. Why it's against the law to libel Idaho potatoes.

There is something plainly dysfunctional about this place, but it is hard to pinpoint. Perhaps it's the isolation and the difficulty of creating networks in a place so hard to travel in: not enough traffic with new ideas moving through. That isolation has led to xenophobia, a fear of strangers or, more precisely, a fear of anyone not white. Certainly in the legislature and in the congressional delegation the problem is easier to define: a paucity of new blood and ideas, much like the cheetahs in Africa that suffer from a lack of new genetic material. And to think we once had Frank Church as senator.

A diverse America with an exciting cultural vibrancy is leaving Idaho quickly, a trend the state cultivates with slogans like "Idaho Is What America Used to Be" and "Welcome to Idaho. Now Go Home!" The first slogan is true when you consider America used to be more sexist, racist, xenophobic, and environmentally unaware.

A recent article in *The New Yorker* touted the amazing comeback of the California economy. In Silicon Valley, where the heart of this economic engine beats, one out of every four employees is foreign born, and the average annual household income of Santa Clara County is more than $100,000. Ten new firms incorporate every day, and there are no laws limiting language to English only.

Diversity contributes to California's bright economy. Forty percent of the working population are Hispanic, the article states, and one of every three foreign-born Latinos can now be considered middle class, with either an annual income above $35,000 or home ownership. What percentage of white Idahoans can claim a similar income?

Many people in Idaho still whine that the state's sorry image is undeserved. The same people will tell you they don't care anyway. That's why they moved here, by God! But many of us with out-of-state relatives have to continually answer questions such as "What the hell is going on up there?" "What's up with those Nazis?"

How do we answer? How do we defend the indefensible?

When I moved to Idaho in 1983, I came for the mountains and rivers. Fifteen years later, I see those same peaks as impenetrable boundaries of isolation and the reflection in the rivers is of a man who longs to return home, home to America.

Burning Zeal
—*Karl Brooks*

"We're always a little afraid." That's what a staunch environmentalist friend told me shortly after I retired from the Idaho legislature and left a big-firm law practice to work for the Idaho Conservation League.

"Afraid of what?" I asked him.

So he patiently explained certain realities of being an environmentalist in an Idaho Panhandle timber town, where the weekly newspaper's editorials read like industry press releases and the county commission tries to defy Forest Service management of national forest lands by passing unconstitutional ordinances.

I thought about my colleague in the Panhandle when I heard about the October 19 arson fire that destroyed a ski lodge and damaged lifts in Vail, Colorado. A radical group called the Earth Liberation Front took credit for the conflagration. He'd taught me that saying unpopular things out loud in certain places held risks we urban Boiseans couldn't really imagine: business boycotts, anonymous phone calls, muttered threats angry enough to carry more than the hint of mayhem.

By speaking out for lower timber cuts, cleaner rivers, and social change, this environmentalist publicly challenged a lot of power. Like many rural Idahoans, he kept raising his voice because he believed the rule of law would keep him and his property safe. He risked being unpopular because the law not only encouraged his protest, it defended his peace against the majority who disliked his view.

Some westerners have tried to justify the crime in Vail by blaming the victim and citing a "higher law" of environmental health. Vail Associates got what it deserved, the argument goes, because it makes obscene profits by abusing public lands and underpaying powerless employees. The company had no legal right to destroy lynx habitat, but it bullied the Forest Service and federal courts into spineless complicity.

This line of reasoning, which the Earth Liberation Front thrill-seekers used to justify their actions, is morally and historically bankrupt. Neither those who lit the match at night, nor those who egged them on by day, cared that their flaming cowardice will make life a little scarier for environmentalists like my brave friend in the Idaho Panhandle. They also failed to see that using criminal violence to push their cause only ups the odds that other zealots, holding very different views about habitat protection on public lands, may strike in the same way.

Progressive reform in the West has depended on extending the law's protection to dissident values. Behind these advances—labor unions for wage workers, civil rights for people of color, even the emergence of healthier attitudes about people's place in nature—are histories too often stained with lawless violence against people who challenged entrenched power. Early this century, workers seeking better pay and conditions in mining and timber industries endured violent attacks by thugs working for employers. Courts, usually beholden to economic kingpins, stood aside. Even the National Guard became a lawless tool for repression: In 1917 in Ludlow, Colorado, mine owners pressured the governor to declare martial law during strikes.

Real progress and dignity came when working people persuaded courts and legislators to grant them basic legal rights to defend their interests, secure their peace, and pursue their share of the American dream. Farm workers in the irrigated West favored peaceful, legal means when they tried to unionize in the 1960s and 1970s. Had they battled employers by burning warehouses at night, they would have forfeited their claims for economic and social justice.

Just as Earth Liberation Front has forfeited any serious moral claim to be advancing "environmental justice" by torching a ski lodge, this act relegates them to the same moral wilderness stalked by Shelly Shannon, who tried to deny women their constitutional rights by terror-bombing family-planning clinics around the West early this decade.

Maybe some future western historian will romantically recall the thugs who torched the Vail lodge as "social bandits," but the history of social change in the real West identifies outrages on all sides instead of taking sides. In the real West we have moved ahead by legalizing and pacifying social conflict, not by justifying violence that serves someone's private definition of a "higher" end.

Anonymous violence in the night, whether bombing Forest Service offices and vehicles in Nevada in the mid-1990s or burning ski lodges in

1998, displays the terrorists' historical ignorance and moral weakness. The real heroes are those westerners who, like my Idaho colleague, are willing to live with a little fear while standing with the law.

Watching the World from Flagstaff

—Mary Sojourner

Three days a week I work in a local bookstore in an Arizona mountain town. Flagstaff was once little more than a wild night on Route 66, a roughneck playground whose saloons were distinctly split between Indian or not, their windows boarded where glass had been taken out by flying bottle or body. The town had more than its share of cheap Chinese restaurants, run by and for the men who laid the rails that still sing through the heart of town. Rogues and solid citizens ate five-cent chow mein and loved the howl of the midnight special.

Those rails are no longer so beloved. Flagstaff's population is no longer mostly cowboys, linemen, and Chinese cooks, nor the more subdued working class place it became. Our town is on its way to being yet another western playpen, a place where the unimaginably wealthy own million-dollar second homes, drive Range Rovers at sixty miles per hour on city streets, cursing the trains that halt them in their busy, busy lives. The "affluent," as they describe themselves modestly, wander from microbrewery to coyote-kitsch boutique to any charming remnant of Old West authenticity, looking for something to fill what can't be filled by mansions, on-line stock-market gambling, or vehicles the size of Shiprock.

A few weeks ago, the people of Turkey were devastated by earthquakes. Tens of thousands of Turks were killed and injured. The town of Adapazari was diminished by 2,800 souls. Golcuk lost all but a handful of buildings, every one of its residents homeless.

Each morning, before driving past Home Depot's clear-cut construction site to the bookstore, I read the on-line news. I tried to imagine how it would be if all of Arizona were shaken as dreadfully as Turkey had been. In a photo of a man trapped alive, his face an inch from the block of concrete that held his head fast, I saw the truth of the absolute power of the earth.

Each morning, each noon I sat at the bookstore desk. The customers bought books on letting go, on millennial revelations channeled from the Pleiades, on the right diet for your blood type. An old woman whose eyes glittered bright as the gold she wore at ears, wrists, and throat asked me what I thought of the blood-type diet book. "Isn't it just so healing?"

"Actually," I said, "I'm not interested in all of that. I think it's impossible to be fully healthy on an ailing planet."

She smiled. "Oh," she said, "you're one of those people who believe in global warming."

"It's not a question of belief," I said. "It's based on scientific fact."

She smiled again. "Well, dear," she said, "I don't know the facts so I just don't believe in it."

Later, a soft-spoken man bought $200 worth of books on Buddhist compassion. He told me he tries to read the news but can't because it upsets him too much. "I have to have my inner calm," he said. "That's my way to heal the earth."

A woman rushed in, eyes wild, holding her right hand out. I prepared to call 911 as she gasped, "I'm new in town. Where's the nail salon? I broke one."

Nobody talked about the earthquake. Nobody.

Seven days. Tens of thousands dead and injured. Seven days in a bookstore that loyal customers call "the heart of Flagstaff." The AIDS support group meets in our big front room. Community activists talk strategy. Six newsletters a month go out from here, on everything from women's issues to bagpiping.

A year ago, when wildfires threatened the boundaries of our upscale suburbs, threatened nothing more than the property of the few and absent, the store and the town were buzzing with fear. A forest thinning project was rushed into action before, many believe, appropriate research considerations were taken. To protect huge and empty mausoleums.

In the last year, one issue generated the most letters to our local paper. Not growth, not the widening income gap between those of us who work here and those we serve, not escalating rents and property "values." What fired us up were the debatable aesthetics of a piece of public art bought and set up on old Route 66.

Seven days and not one customer mentioned the earthquake.

Nor did I. I waited. I was doing appropriate research. I thought of the Turkish man, his face an inch from his death. Waiting. And the couple trapped under their bed, a floor below where they had been sleeping. "We didn't know," they said, "if each breath was our last."

Days later, another Turkish tremor kills one and injures dozens. Wildfires scorch the West. I wonder what I will hear on the streets of the town I keep loving. Devastation or property damage? Have we been numbed by too many disasters? Or our great good American luck? Or have too many of us New Westerners simply forgotten that the irrevocable power in our playground can, in a thirty-second shudder, make us kin to our distant neighbors?

Home on the Whitening Range
—Richard Manning

One does not expect enlightenment from a barbershop conversation, but there it was. I'd always had hunches about the nature of demographic change in western mountain towns, nasty hunches, hunches counter to the conventional wisdom that immigration was motivated by the newcomers' love of the land, so the newcomers would become allies in environmental struggles. Nothing, however, explained my skepticism, other than the simple fact that the political struggles of my place steadily grew harder and meaner, despite the newcomers.

The woman in the barbershop was prattling on about the charms of Missoula, Montana, my hometown, her new hometown.

"It's just like a little San Francisco."

I baited: "So is that where you're from?"

"No, L.A., but it's like a little San Francisco here."

"Well, actually, no. It's all white. No ethnic diversity, and San Francisco is nothing if not diverse. This place is all white."

"I know. Isn't it wonderful?"

Did I mention the newcomer was white? Of course not. Didn't need to. They almost all are.

I offer here another name for the migration of coastal urbanites into the mountain towns of the Rockies and Cascadia: white flight. Writing in March in *The New York Times*, California journalist Dale Maharidge offered this observation: "California is now essentially one large urban core, with the intermountain West as its suburb."

He says that's how it feels from his end in Palo Alto, and that's how it feels from mine in Missoula. A majority of Californians now are not white. As immigrants grow wealthy enough to afford suburban homes, the white flight that built the suburbs in the first place flees on.

So now that we have a name for it, what does it mean? Folks who analyze the primary changes of America during the last decade mark them by the impoverishment of both cities and rural areas, then talk about a rural-urban split. The poverty is right, but the split is wrong; this analysis misses the point, and it misses more than half of the U.S. population, which is neither rural nor urban but suburban. This majority is a new one, its emergence the dominant factor of American politics in this generation. Suburbanites gave us Ronald Reagan and his spawn. The same force erased John Kennedy's question about what we can do for our country and replaced it with the legitimized greed present in Reagan's pivotal question: "Are you better off today than you were four years ago?"

What Maharidge believes this portends for mountain towns like mine is increasingly conservative politics. My state, for instance, once the most Democratic of the intermountain West, can no longer seem to elect a Democrat. True enough, there has always been a large conservative element in the state, like Washington's and Oregon's, based in its eastern agricultural half, ranchers and farmers, not newcomers. As of the last elections, though, there was not a single Democrat in Flathead County in any elected office, and Flathead is among the three fastest-growing counties in the state, on the west side, a glitz county, a magnet for immigrants. Maharidge is right.

I worry about what this new conservative, suburban force portends for environmental politics, as opposed to pure partisan politics. Remember, we were counting on the newcomers for some help. So what sort of help might they give? It depends on what one means by environmental politics.

What I mean by environmentalism is the growing understanding that the earth is finite and intricate, that it supports our existence here only to the degree we respect its limits and preserve its intricacy. Pondering this fundamental can quickly bring one to the conclusion that life will be grim indeed for most of the world's six billion souls if a few go on consuming resources at literally twenty times the rate of the rest.

Suburban America is not about respecting limits.

The rubber-stamped chain malls have begun to ring my city, monuments to the founding fact of suburban existence, which is consumption. The sports utes stream down the valley highway that flees the city to the gridlock of new trophy homes with arched windows craning to steal a vantage of the horizon's unspoiled peaks. All of this seems to say "I got mine."

Where is the recognition of limits here that will bring on the real sacrifices necessary to preserve the very wilderness and wildlife those arching windows want to see?

Of course, there is another view of environmental politics, one evolved from the legitimate fear of poisons, but one that eventually distills that fear to the point it can only be understood with the subject "I." This explains why so many of those gas-guzzling sport utes can be found parked at the local health food store. The acronym that covers this branch of environmentalism is NIMBY-ism, a belief that a problem is not a problem unless it occurs in your own backyard, but it's okay if the effects of your consumption foul someone else's backyard. This is the companion sentiment to "I got mine." I expect to hear a good deal more about it.

How the Farm Bureau Lost Its Overalls

—Susan Zakin

Do you know who your Farm Bureau is?

I understand. This doesn't seem as important as your kid's soccer tournament or the fact that it's almost tax time again. But it is. In fact, you might be a member of your state Farm Bureau and not even know it because the Farm Bureau isn't a bunch of guys in overalls sitting around Mom's Café talking about wheat prices.

The Farm Bureau today is the equivalent of a giant multinational corporation, only it doesn't have to pay taxes. Various state farm bureaus own marketing cooperatives that are raking in profits and stifling family farms; *Fortune* magazine recently ranked the American Farm Bureau Federation the seventeenth most effective lobbyist in Washington, D.C. About 95 percent of the Farm Bureau's 4.7 million members aren't farmers. They're customers of the group's many insurance companies, sixty-three of which earn a total of more than $6.5 billion annually in net premiums.

Once you know this, it's less surprising that Farm Bureau policies sound as if they are written by a combination of oil company CEOs and the Montana Freemen. The Farm Bureau supports voluntary prayer in public schools; transferring federal land, except parks and wildlife refuges, to the states, and halting U.S. funding to the United Nations. The group opposes the global warming treaty signed in Kyoto. If Farm Bureau policies went into effect tomorrow, ten-year-olds would be allowed to work.

Small farmers across the country have been seething at the group's tilt toward agribusiness and big oil. The seething was quiet until last week, when the Washington, D.C.–based environmental group Defenders of Wildlife went public with the charge that the farmer has no overalls.

Defenders has been warring with the Farm Bureau over endangered species reintroduction all over the country. The Farm Bureau is winning right now, so Defenders went on the offensive, showing up at the organization's annual conference in Albuquerque with a tame gray wolf named Rami who licked people's faces and rather unceremoniously urinated on the carpet of the Hyatt Regency Hotel but failed to maul any small children, dogs, or frail elderly folks.

Wolves are important, but I'm more concerned that the Farm Bureau doesn't pay taxes. In 1993, the Internal Revenue Service ruled that dues from nonfarming members had to be taxed, which would have cost the Farm Bureau about $32 million a year. Representative David Camp, a Michigan Republican, came to the rescue with the Tax Fairness for Agriculture Act of 1996. Camp and many of the bill's 126 cosponsors received $109,824 from political action committees affiliated with state farm bureaus, according to investigative reporter Vicki Monks in *Defenders* magazine.

The way I see it, the Farm Bureau is bucking for an identity crisis similar to the one wracking the National Rifle Association. Several years ago, the NRA veered so sharply to the crackpot right—calling federal agents "jack-booted thugs" in a fund-raising letter—that it alienated many long-time members.

The Farm Bureau is headed down the same road. In 1995, Mark Dalpiaz, a young Colorado farmer, wrote a letter to his local farm bureau complaining that the group was one step away from neo-Nazism. What does school prayer have to do with farming, anyway? "Are the only real farmers fundamentalist Christians?" wrote Dalpiaz.

More recently, Missouri farmer Scott Dye blasted the Farm Bureau's support for factory hog farms, which hurt family hog farmers and are believed to contribute to outbreaks of *Pfiesteria piscicida*, a highly toxic microbe that kills fish and can make people sick.

"We've lost 5,000 independent swine producers in Missouri in the last five years—family farms—and they're gone forever. The Farm Bureau stood by and let that happen," Dye told reporter Monks. "If these people lose their prestige as the spokesmen for agriculture, they're just another insurance lobby, and insurance lobbies are a dime a dozen."

Mike Callicrate, a Kansas feedlot operator, and Leo McDonell, a Montana rancher, are traveling the heartland speaking out against international free trade, as well as the high profits of beef middlemen. Crowds cheer when Leo McDonell asks "Why are we worried about the predators in Yellowstone Park, when the biggest predator is right here? It's the packers, and the Farm Bureau has cleared the way for them."

Reform won't be easy. The NRA relies on its members for dues and support. The Farm Bureau, on the other hand, makes so much money from its business ventures that it will be tough for people like Mike Callicrate or

Scott Dye to have an impact. Yet they're probably the only ones who can change things. After all, they're farmers—so they can vote.

Or they can just clear a space on the carpet for Rami.

The Politics of Hate and Switch
—*Dan Dagget*

In a world where kids shoot kids, and we blow one another up over nothing more than politics, I've had it with people who peddle hate.

And because I'm an environmentalist, I've especially had it with groups who exploit my concern about the environment to try to sell me such poison. That's why, after twenty years of participating in a war of loaded words from both sides of the environmental debate, I decided to do something different.

The other day, when I read a solicitation from an environmental group that used the racist-sounding smear "welfare ranchers" and asked me to send them money "to stop the billion dollar rip-off of our tax dollars," I made two calls.

First, I called a specialist in hate crimes at Northern Arizona University. I asked her if "welfare ranchers"really was an example of hate language.

"I'd call it classist rather than racist," she said, "but it's still hate."

Then I called the local Forest Service office and asked, "What are you doing to waste so much of my money subsidizing ranchers?"

Since the Forest Service and Bureau of Land Management spend more money administering grazing on public lands than they collect in fees from ranchers whose cattle graze those lands (and since the ranchers sell those cattle at a profit), we say this constitutes a subsidy. So I expected an answer such as "We're building fences and killing predators for ranchers, and we're spending tons of money restoring the lands their animals have overgrazed."

Instead, the answer I got was "Mostly, we're responding to lawsuits, appeals of grazing management plans, letters of intent to sue—stuff like that."

How does that subsidize ranchers, I wondered? Even though these actions are directed at the government, ranchers have to hire lawyers to represent them, have to prove they didn't do whatever the suits charge, and have to attend the interminable meetings that go with such things. That's an expense, not a subsidy.

Other offices around the West gave me the same answer: Government land managers are spending a huge amount of their time dealing with environmental litigation. "Eighty percent of my time is spent dealing with conflict,"said one forest supervisor in Arizona, who estimated that two-thirds of his range staff's time was being consumed by one lawsuit.

A range conservationist in southern Arizona laughed when I asked how often she monitored the ranches under her charge. "All I do is push papers," she said. I received similar responses from workers for both the Forest Service and the Bureau of Land Management in Montana, Colorado, Nevada, and Utah. Those government workers also told me that the majority of these actions are filed by the same groups that use the "welfare rancher" smear.

That's when I realized that what we have here is a case of "hate and switch." The same people who have been manipulating us with hate words are the ones who are really benefiting from the subsidies they smear others for receiving.

This is how it works: When federal range staffers respond to legal actions brought by pressure groups, they're benefiting the groups, not the ranchers. How do we know this? Because, as government workers process those lawsuits, they're creating a product the pressure groups market to their members. "Look at how effectively we're protecting your public lands,"the groups trumpet. "Look at how many lawsuits we've filed! Send us money!"

In this way, pressure groups are able to charge their own obstructionist activities against their opponents' accounts. What a scam! The more money they force the government to spend, the worse their opponents look. The measure of victory here is not how many lawsuits you win, but how many you file. Groups on both sides of environmental issues use this tactic. Just as environmental groups use it to smear ranchers and loggers, "wise-use"groups use it to discredit endangered species recovery and similar activities.

When properly used, litigation is a valuable tool for addressing environmental problems. When twisted into a scam that enables peddlers of hate and divisiveness to belly up to the federal trough and become bloated with subsidized power, however, lawsuits do not mend ecosystems, restore biodiversity, or sustain communities. They promote money-gobbling court battles, frustrated federal land managers, and a

West more balkanized with every lawsuit.

Pitting us against one another, the Hate and Switchers keep us from developing the one tool that can lift us out of this quagmire: cooperation.

Biting the Hand That Feeds
—Pat Williams

Whenever I hear a pundit or politician in the West spouting about the need to transfer power from the federal government to the states, I think back to my college days at the University of Montana.

The campus is bordered on its northwest by the Clark Fork River, which, in the days of my youth, was an open sewer. Under the auspices of the city and state through which it flowed, the river was abused and ignored until it actually became a menace. A caring but exasperated public finally petitioned the federal government to clean the waterway—much as the citizens of Ohio were to do when the Cuyahoga River actually caught on fire!

Today the Clark Fork, the Cuyahoga, and many hundreds of other American rivers run clear because after 200 years of mistaken trust in our localities and states to ensure clean, safe water, the citizens finally demanded that their federal government aggressively assert itself as an environmental partner with our states and cities. The wonderful results of the federal response are everywhere.

The truth is the West needs a strong federal government, perhaps more than any other region in the country.

Oh, I know, that sounds almost un-American in a country that, at least for now, harbors a popular fetish to harangue anything federal. The current anti-federal mongering, particularly by the Far Right, is not only wrongheaded, it is dangerous. And it threatens to upset the balance—what Supreme Court Justice Sandra Day O'Connor refers to as "the elegant balance"—between our state and federal governments.

That balance was purposefully hardwired into the United States Constitution by America's founders, who brilliantly recognized that the sharing of authority among state and federal governments would allow each to make its separate contribution to the building and sustaining of the country and its citizens. It is called federalism and it works.

Consider just one element—costs. For those of us living in the lightly populated West, the costs of essential public services are critical. The equitable absorption of costs through the federal treasury has saved many western states' bacon. Can 900,000 Montanans pay the cost of the many hundreds of miles of interstate highways and bridges that cross and link our state? Will the 500,000 citizens of Wyoming be financially responsible for the Pell grants and federally guaranteed student loans that assist their 20,000 college-bound students?

If left to operate alone, our state governments, particularly here in the West, would be in the deepest of trouble. And, frankly, the duplication, confusion, disarray, regulations, and—yes—fraud, waste, and abuse in state governments, taken collectively, make the workings of Washington, D.C., look almost efficient by comparison. Those who doubt that should ask the nation's long-distance truckers or railroaders. They, and many other interstate businesses, will tell you that state, and often local, governments are their biggest regulatory nightmare.

State governments in the West cannot satisfy the basic safety, health care, transportation, or even education requirements of their own people. Failing that, they can hardly find the vitality to be the vaunted "laboratories of change" we have heard so much about.

We also hear a lot about "devolution"—the effort to further empower state governments with authority now reserved mostly for the federal government. The idea has some basis and reason for support, but as we move toward devolution, let's be clearheaded about the intent of our founders as well as the inherent weakness of states acting alone. States and state's rightists have too often ignored the civil rights of their own citizens and, even more so, the rights of their citizens to live in relatively clean and safe environments.

Our founding fathers somehow knew that our rights as individuals are best ensured by not being beholden to only one government. Thus they built in the checks and balances inherent in the partnership of federal and state governments. No people anywhere have benefited more from that federalism than have we westerners. As we consider this new movement toward more jurisdiction and authority to the states, we should do so with caution, wisdom, and a good memory.

Unleashing the Power of Rivers
—Bruce Babbitt

Some eras are born to instant acclaim. Others emerge quietly, gathering strength over time, before leaping onto the national stage.

We are in the midst of one of those bold, new leaps in the management of America's rivers. Not since the start of the great dam-building era during the 1930s, in fact, have we encountered anything this significant.

I am comfortable making this pronouncement because, as U.S. Secretary of Interior, I am a participant in this movement myself, an emcee to history. Four times in thirteen months now, I have swung ceremonial sledgehammers to celebrate something monumental on the American landscape: the destruction of environmentally harmful dams.

You read that right: The U.S. Department of Interior, after helping supervise the most intensive flurry of dam building in world history, is changing course. Today, we and other branches of the federal government are encouraging the selective destruction of certain dams, public and private, that cause exceptional environmental damage.

Congress is not yet with us, but perhaps one day it will be, for what's igniting this movement is not the federal bureaucracy. It is community spirit. It is rice farmers, utility company officials, civic boosters, fishermen, conservationists, aquatic biologists, Native Americans, and others. Together these Americans are finding promise, not peril, in the unleashing of rivers. By removing dams, they are diversifying their economies, healing watersheds, reducing Endangered Species Act headaches, and restoring beauty, vigor, and recreation to their downtown centers.

Perhaps that is why each new event on this dam-busting tour brings larger, more supportive crowds, more media attention. But what is it about the sound of a sledgehammer that so seizes the imagination?

I believe two things are at work. Number one—an era is winding down. Until the 1990s, Interior secretaries dedicated dams; they sang their praises. They genuflected to dollars, development, and politics. Today, we recognize other forms of commerce—such as self-sustaining salmon runs—in our nation's rivers, and we find growing, broad-based constituencies arguing on their behalf.

The other thing is basic: We overdid it. There are 75,000 dams six feet high and over in America. Think about that number. Seventy-five thousand dams means we have been building, on average, one dam a day, including weekends, since the Declaration of Independence. Pardon the phrase—but we overdosed. Dams justified for their economic value gave way to dams built with taxpayer subsidies, dams draped in political pork, dams clouded by dubious if not deceitful cost-benefit projections.

This is neither hyperbole nor partisan rhetoric. This is reality. Today, we are paying the price for our dam habit. We have obliterated fish-spawning runs, caused the extinction of some species, transformed rivers into watermains, irrigation canals, and slack-water sumps, robbed our estuaries and deltas of much-needed nutrients, stolen sediment from our ocean beaches, debased a part of our American heritage. At the same time, flood control—one of the main reasons for building many big dams—has become, in many areas, something of a joke. Flood damage in America has increased, not decreased, despite billions invested in big dams.

Does this mean I support tearing down all, most, or even many dams? Of course not. But I believe we should challenge dam owners every-where—including the U.S. Bureau of Reclamation and the Army Corps of Engineers—to demonstrate by hard facts, not sentiment and myth, that a dam's continued operation is in the public interest. Often, this will mean adopting more environmentally friendly operating regimens, such as we have done at Arizona's Glen Canyon Dam to begin to restore the Colorado River through Grand Canyon National Park. In some cases, it will mean actual removal of dams themselves.

Remember, dams are not monuments. They are not pyramids. They are tools that serve the needs of the people who oversee them. Those needs change, often quite rapidly, over the course of a generation.

Most dams were built decades ago with no consideration of their envi-ronmental, recreational, or spiritual costs. Our challenge today is to find a new equilibrium—one that balances economic benefits with other intan-gible goods and services, one that evaluates dams by the health of the watersheds and the people to which they belong.

Often, in thinking of dams and rivers, I am reminded of Ecclesiastes:

One generation passeth away
and another generation cometh
but the Earth abideth always.
All rivers runneth to the sea
yet the sea is not full;
to the place where the rivers flow
there they flow again.

A beautiful passage, but a chilling one, too. For today, it no longer rings true. The mighty Colorado River no longer reaches the sea—due to the many dams across its course. Other rivers arrive feeble and anemic, vastly depleted of biological life, stripped of their majesty. That is a shame. As one generation passeth into another, the future of our rivers rests firmly in our hands.

Dam Culture
—*Rocky Barker*

When Governor Cecil Andrus destroyed the Lewiston Dam on Idaho's Clearwater River in the 1980s, almost no one called him a radical.

The dam had long passed its useful life. Although it had a fish ladder, the tattered structure was a continuing impediment to the migration of salmon and steelhead to and from spawning grounds upstream. In addition to its economic value, the emotional ties to the Lewiston Dam were frayed and worn.

Now a national movement is building to reassess the values of dams built over the last century. The Federal Energy Regulatory Commission ordered the Edwards Dam in Maine removed. The Department of Interior is only awaiting the okay of Congress to begin removing two dams on Washington's Elwha River.

The U.S. Army Corps of Engineers is preparing an environmental impact statement on breaching four dams on the lower Snake River in Washington to prevent the extinction of the same Snake River salmon and steelhead Andrus's dam-busting aimed to save.

The movement grows out of a recognition that rivers and the watersheds that sustain them are interconnected ecosystems with biological limits few recognized when the dams were built. Blocking or changing the flows of rivers like the Colorado and Columbia threatens the very fabric of these water webs of life.

Yet without these dams millions of acres of western desert would not be verdant farmlands. Billions of dollars of wealth would not trickle through the economy in electric lines, vital wartime industries, and metropolitan housing developments.

Industrial icons such as Harry Morrison built the dams and political heroes such as Franklin Roosevelt dedicated them. They are more than just concrete and dollars to the people who grew up in their shadow. They are a shrine to our ability to wrestle control from nature for the common good.

That's why no scientific or economic argument will sway many of the benefactors of the dams and the federal programs that built them. It's not just an issue of science, economics, or even sociology. It's about culture and values.

How tightly the benefactors of the dams hold on to their own cultural values can be seen in their attempt to attach the radical label to anyone who would suggest reevaluating the need for dams.

The newspaper I work for, *The Idaho Statesman,* was an early contributor to the movement when it called for breaching the four Snake dams in a series of three editorials. Breaching them means removing the earthen sections of the four dams, allowing the river to return to its natural level and flow while leaving the concrete structure high and dry.

The Statesman's editorial made the case that breaching the dams was likely the only way to keep Idaho's salmon from going extinct. It also said breaching would save taxpayers money and ultimately help the region economically.

Since I did the research that helped the newspaper make its case, I think all of the arguments are defensible. As a reporter, I also recognize they are arguable.

One of the best political arguments against removing any dams is that once environmentalists get started they won't stop. Each success will be a model for the next campaign. In a region that has watched public-land logging dramatically reduced by endangered species protection, grazing cutbacks, and other environmentally generated restrictions, this idea sticks.

Yet I hear almost no environmentalist suggesting we get rid of all dams or even most of them. Fly fishermen (myself included) have become enamored with the tailrace fisheries below dams on the Henry's Fork of the Snake River, the Green, the Bighorn, and other storied streams of the West. Before removing any dam, proponents must make the case that it is biologically necessary and economically feasible, but they will also have to recognize the cultural and emotional ties to dams.

That is why the best way to address these issues is from the ground up, not the top down. Local watershed councils ought to be the first forum for serious debate on whether a dam should go or stay. When the watershed is the entire Snake or Columbia Basin, it gets more complicated, but the rationale is the same. Level heads will rule the day if the community is allowed to get fully involved in the process.

I recently talked to an ardent, but thoughtful, dam supporter, who told me that he is not convinced yet that removing the Snake River dams will save the salmon runs. I expected that stance, but he caught me by surprise when he said he would reverse his position and join the environmentalists if the scientific evidence ever shows that there is no alternative.

A small admission, perhaps, but one that packs a strong message for everyone involved with the dam-removal debate: A little bending will keep our culture and our rivers from breaking.

The Greening of the Rednecks
—*Mark Matthews*

Environmentalism is a dirty word in many parts of the rural West. Some small-town residents can hardly spit out words like "Sierra Club" without placing an expletive before them. Yet when it comes to crunch time when they are threatened by mines, clear-cuts, or dams, many of these same rugged individuals jump to the defense of their own backyards.

It's a wonderful paradox.

In Montana, grassroots groups have stopped construction of a dam at Kootenai Falls, helped shut down a vat-leach cyanide mill above Pony, Montana, stopped gold mining in the Sweet Grass Hills and oil and gas exploration along the Rocky Mountain Front.

No professional environmentalists need apply here. The ranks include ranchers, schoolteachers, laborers, businessmen, farmers, outfitters, and housewives—in other words, the man and woman next door. Call them the Little Browns in honor of their grassroots approach.

"Local grassroots groups are critically important to the environmental movement,"Aimee Boulanger of the Mineral Policy Center in Bozeman, Montana, told me. "[Big Green] environmental groups have obvious shortcomings. They can get stretched between several regional or national issues, while grassroots groups can truly focus on one issue that impacts their backyards."

When a power company wanted to build a dam below Kootenai Falls near Troy, Montana, local citizens formed the Cabinet Resources Group. They stopped the project dead in its tracks. Today, the falls are one of the region's largest tourist attractions. Now, the group is working to prevent ASARCO from mining under the Cabinet Mountains Wilderness and even has a majority of the county commissioners on its side.

According to spokesman Cesar Hernandez, a log crafter from Heron, Montana, a large national group couldn't have galvanized the community to fight such projects.

"People know who you are and what you stand for," he told me.

In 1989, when miners wanted to dig for gold in the Sweet Grass Hills in north-central Montana, local ranchers, like Arlo Skari, started getting nervous. "We realized our water supplies would be gone," Skari said. "Plus, there was plenty of Native American religious use of the area, as well as plenty of wildlife. We love our hills."

A core group of about ten activists circulated information throughout the surrounding communities, urging people to attend scoping meetings. Their opposition managed to prevent the drilling of thirty-six exploratory holes. Later, with the help of residents from the nearby Blackfeet Reservation, they convinced Secretary of Interior Bruce Babbitt to withdraw the area from mining consideration.

"Although most [of the local residents] are Republicans, they were almost all against mining in the hills," Skari said.

A more informal group surfaced more than twenty years ago when oil and gas companies began eyeballing Montana's Rocky Mountain Front for exploratory drilling. The loose-knit group, known as Friends of the Rocky Mountain Front, is composed of ranchers, farmers, outfitters, business-people, and professionals in small towns stretching from the Blackfeet Reservation south to Helena, Montana. It's a motley crew, according to Gene Sentz, a schoolteacher and part-time guide in Choteau, Montana. "Some would cringe about being called environmentalists," he told me.

A couple of years ago, members of the network wrote many letters during a public comment period on proposed oil and gas drilling along the front that helped sway Forest Service officials to deny leases for the area.

Over time, attitudes change. Enemies become allies. Years ago, if you went into a bar in Pony, Montana, you'd likely hear conversations peppered with phrases like "those damn environmentalists." That all began to change when a mining outfit built a cyanide mill above the town that threatened to contaminate local water wells.

"When we had to come out of the closet, so to speak, I don't think any of us were part of an environmental group," said Janet Zimmerman, whose grandfather had taught school in Pony. "I like to think the town is now in a state of healing. A number of us now belong to environmental groups and have found a new calling."

Skari has also noticed a change in attitude around the Sweet Grass Hills where residents recently strongly supported an initiative that banned cyanide gold mines in Montana. "People have quit attacking the government and environmental groups," he said. "They now are suspicious of corporations."

There's a lesson here for the Big Greens. Don't count out the local guys and gals, no matter how red their necks appear. When push comes to shove, chances are, they're not going to let their backyards turn into cesspools or industrial parks. Now that's great news for all of us.

Running and Losing
—Charles Pezeshki

My environmentalist friends warned me about running for public office. "Don't do it," they said, "As an outspoken environmental activist you are already a public figure. Getting elected would just subject your visionary ideas to the messy and compromising world of politics and undermine your credibility."

But no one else was going to run for the local state senate seat in our small, supposedly progressive county in Idaho, one of the most conservative states in the Union. So I filled out my petition, delivered a fire-and-brimstone speech to the local Democrats, and sent it to the secretary of state's elections office. The local Democrats rallied around my campaign: I had fire in my belly, issues that I cared about, even if I was unsure if I had the stomach for elected political office.

The Democratic cadres down south in Boise weren't nearly as supportive. My opponent, a local hide, fur, and wild animal parts dealer, was one of the few moderate Republicans in the state legislature. He actually supported abortion rights and had the best environmental voting record in his party. Nothing to brag about, especially in anti-Green Idaho, but he wasn't the devil incarnate. He had Democratic friends in the legislature, one ex-labor leader who recommended that the state branch of the AFL-CIO endorse him, which they did, even though my opponent refused to come out against right-to-work, union-busting legislation. So much for labor politics in Idaho.

Upon winning the primary in May, I was bombarded by every special- and public-interest group in the state. I was amazed how even groups of people I hadn't tried to reach with my environmental activism were imbued with the myth of a people-hating environmentalist. Few were interested in giving me money, especially such campaign donation stalwarts as the timber, mining, and ranching industries.

The bluegrass growers sent me a nice letter, saying that if I would just come out in favor of voluntary—as opposed to mandatory—burning standards (a hot topic in our state), a donation to my campaign war chest (not exactly bursting to the seams with $400 total) could be arranged. I declined.

I was a reluctant candidate. I didn't go door to door looking for votes. I only sat one day at the county fair, shaking hands and talking to people. I didn't even get my official campaign brochure together until a month before the election. The extent of my paid advertising was one big media drop—an insert in a local newspaper.

My opponent, on the other hand, spent over $10,000 on his campaign. He knocked on doors. He spent the week at the fair. He also took to delivering ad hominem attacks at the various forums—the League of Women Voters debates, the Chamber of Commerce presentations. After the first forum, he ended up being reprimanded by the opinions editors at the regional paper for attempting to paint me with the usual Earth First! label.

I didn't take it lying down—but fighting back was unproductive, and for once I truly understood how hard it is to talk about issues in a political race. Responses at debates were always only one minute long, hardly enough time to detail complicated policy positions. My opponent, no master of the sound bite or progressive policy on most issues, repeated platitudes to the masses, along the usual line of "balance between the environment and jobs."

In the end, I lost. I had expected this, of course. What I had not expected was the 35 percent of the vote I received, nor the two precincts that I actually won. People I had never met walked up to me in the supermarket, told me that they had voted for me, and thanked me for running, fully aware of my Green background.

Just by running, I forced Republicans to spend money against me, thus helping another Democrat over the top in a tight race with another incumbent Republican in our district. By garnering a significant vote tally, as well as appearing and assisting with other statewide political races, I showed the state Democratic party at large that Greens in Idaho could be both a force and an asset.

It was no fun running for state office, but I discovered lots of ground ceded to the opposition without a fight in our local community organizations and business groups. If environmental issues are going to be a factor in political races, local candidates must run on them as part of their platform—which means environmentalists must run, as

Democrats, Independents, or Greens. It humanizes us. And if you run, you can't be ignored.

I'm glad I didn't take my friends' advice.

Invisible Democrats
—*Daniel Kemmis*

I happened to be on the East Coast during the 1998 elections, where I heard a leading Democratic tactician comment that Democrats now had the chance in the year 2000 to consolidate and advance the gains made in the on-the-road-to-becoming-solidly-Republican South.

Emboldened by this mention of regional politics, I asked if Democrats were concerned about the tightening Republican grip on the West. After all, Democrats lost the governorships of Nebraska, Colorado, and Nevada in 1998. While Democratic governors sit in Missouri and Iowa, and in the Pacific Coast states, fully three-quarters of the congressional districts in the interior West are now held by Republicans.

"There isn't anybody there," this hard-boiled New Democrat replied. "There are fewer electoral votes in the interior West than in Pennsylvania. We have to concentrate our attention where the votes are."(It would actually take only six of the West's least populous states— Alaska, Montana, Wyoming, Idaho, Utah, and New Mexico—to add up to Pennsylvania's twenty-three electoral votes, but the point is taken—and quite resentfully—by westerners.)

The overwhelming presence of public lands in the West goes far to account for the Republican hegemony of the region. Democrats are seen, correctly, as the party most supportive of the national government's domination of the West, while the Republican Party is perceived as committed to giving westerners some meaningful control of their own beloved landscape. If democracy implies trust in the people to manage their own affairs, the Democrats can only appear as the undemocratic party in the West because they never tire of telling westerners "We absolutely do not trust you to care for the place you have chosen to inhabit."

Take, for example, the proposal for a congressionally mandated zero-cut policy on public lands. This campaign, which would halt all commercial logging on national forests, is coordinated by thirteen environmental groups, including the Sierra Club, Native Forest Network, John Muir Project, and Inland Empire Public Lands Council. In spite of its veneer of bipartisan sponsorship, the National Forest Protection and Restoration Act is a Democratic bill: Of its thirty-one cosponsors, only two are Republicans. Not surprisingly, none of the sponsors are from the interior West or from any district dominated by public lands.

This approach to environmental issues still has great appeal to national environmental groups, who find in it not only a way to advance what appears to them to be good environmental policy but also an effective way to build membership around an emotionally appealing position. However, in the West, where many small communities are still dependent on timber production from public lands, this is just one more instance of nonwesterners (mostly Democrats) trying to exercise a kind of imperial dominion over western landscapes and communities.

I guess I shouldn't be surprised that Democrats still cling to this approach since westerners essentially don't exist in the tactical calculations of the National Democratic Party. "There's nobody there," at least not by comparison to the rich harvests of nonwestern environmentalists residing in states without national forests but with many electoral votes.

National environmental groups reward those congressional and presidential candidates (again mostly Democrats) whose votes support the extension of the nationalist approach. This gains votes and contributions for Democrats outside the West, but within the region it contributes to the party's steady decline. So far, the Democrats have found the tradeoff acceptable, if not positively beneficial. Given Vice President Gore's high standing with (and responsiveness to) national environmentalists, we have to expect this same strategy to be carried into the 2000 campaign.

It may take the Democrats losing the White House in 2000 to persuade them to rethink this approach. If they do lose it, they will almost certainly find themselves reviewing an electoral college map with essentially no Democratic votes from the interior West. Then, perhaps, the Democrats will begin to ask whether it is good politics to write off an entire region.

Super Saturday in the West?
—Ed Quillen

Governors from the Mountain West recently gathered in Salt Lake City to endorse and promote a regional presidential primary in 2000.

Their political logic is fairly simple, along the lines of "monkey see, monkey do." The monkey they have observed is that portion of the United States on the nether side of the Mason-Dixon line.

The South, even though it is not America's richest or most populous region, swings a big stick in national politics. The president is from Arkansas, the senate majority leader is from Mississippi, the new speaker of the House of Representatives is from Louisiana, and he replaced one from Georgia.

In other words, schoolchildren might be forgiven for thinking that it was Grant who surrendered to Lee at Appomattox in 1865.

Political scholars attribute much of this Confederate power to the invention of "Super Tuesday"—a day in March of presidential election years when many Southern states hold primaries.

A relatively small state like Arkansas or South Carolina would not get much attention on its own. When adjoining states are holding primaries at the same time, then the candidates can find time to visit and get their speechwriters and spin doctors to fabricate material that addresses regional concerns.

Thus the candidate who whistles "Dixie" best gains an early edge, which translates into easier fund-raising, more advertising, and often enough delegate votes for the nomination.

Our governors want the Mountain West to get the same sort of attention with a "Super Saturday." Eight states—Colorado, Arizona, Idaho, Wyoming, Nevada, New Mexico, Utah, and Arizona—would hold their presidential primary elections or delegate-selection caucuses on the first Saturday after the first Tuesday in March. The selected date falls between two bigger events—after the California and New York primaries and before the southern Super Tuesday.

The mechanics seem simple enough, but what happens next? We can assume that no Democrat with more than a spoonful of brains will bother with our primary, since the Mountain West is the most reliably Republican part of the country. So if we do gain a bigger role in presidential selection, it will be the Republican candidate.

Then suppose that our candidate—we'll call him Max Rypland—were nominated and elected, all because he addressed the expressed political concerns of the Mountain West. Shortly after the inauguration, then, we might be reading stories like this:

"President Max Rypland yesterday announced several legislative proposals and executive actions concerning the Mountain West, which he praised as 'the most American part of America, where the American Dream is an abiding reality.'

"The president said he will instruct the U.S. Fish and Wildlife Service to halt enforcement of the Endangered Species Act, whose repeal he will seek. Instead, he added, the federal government will offer bounties of up to $1,000 per pelt for the Canadian lynx, black-footed ferret, Mexican gray wolf, and grizzly bear.

"In a related announcement, Interior Secretary Helen Chenoweth (of Idaho fame) said power production will be maximized at Glen Canyon Dam, where an infantry battalion will be permanently stationed 'to protect this national resource from subversive terrorists.'

"Chenoweth also said she was instructing the U.S. Bureau of Reclamation to dust off some long-abandoned plans and to begin issuing contracts for dam construction at Hells Canyon, Echo Park, Bridge Canyon, and Marble Gorge.

"The latter two would flood the bottom of the Grand Canyon, but Chenoweth said the resulting lakes would 'make the vistas of the canyon more accessible to the great majority of Americans, who are pressed for time, as opposed to the unemployed tree huggers who don't do anything productive anyway.'

"As for trees, Forest Service Chief Craig Thomas (of Wyoming) said he will soon announce the biggest timber sale of all time—all 190 million acres of the entire national-forest system. 'The current system of public ownership is just socialism, and that's a failed doctrine,' he said. 'By selling it all to the highest bidder, American free enterprise will make it more productive to the benefit of all citizens.'

"Back at the White House, President Rypland answered a reporter's question about the bulge under his suit coat by pulling out a .357 revolver, then shooting out a bulb on an overhead chandelier. 'In case any of you are already looking,' he joked, 'here's the smoking gun for this administration.' "

A president beholden to the Mountain West after our special regional primary in 2000? As the saying goes, be careful what you wish for, because you might get it.

Craig Versus Craig: May the Best Man Win
—*Ed Marston*

According to Phil Burgess, the human brain starts working at birth and does not stop until the subject of public lands comes up.

Burgess is a policy wonk of the first order, and as head of the Center for the New West, he loves to throw conferences—on the New West's economy, on its politics, and so on. Until his ACCESS 2000 conference in February, he had avoided public-lands issues. He sees grazing and logging and endangered species as black holes that suck in energy without yielding light.

Burgess, who recently took a job with telecommunications giant US West, seems to have thrown ACCESS 2000 because he believes that a Nixon-in-China scenario may be emerging in the interior West. "Nixon" is Larry Craig, the three-term Republican senator from Idaho who is the best friend the timber industry, the dam operators, and the dirt bikers ever had. He is also the "father" of the Salvage Logging Rider—the West's most notorious law of the 1990s, which gave the timber industry yet another whack at public forests.

Craig, therefore has impeccable anti-environmental credentials, just as Richard Nixon had impeccable anti-Communist credentials. That may make Craig the perfect person to break the century-old pattern of enmity between conservation and western extractive interests.

It is a pattern set in motion by Teddy Roosevelt, who created the national forests and enraged the West in the early 1900s. It was continued by Jimmy Carter, who protected land in Alaska and enraged the West in the 1970s. It was perfected by Bill Clinton, who is creating national monuments and enraging the West in the 1990s. These presidents anger some westerners, but they gain reputations as conservationists and win votes across the nation.

In reaction, the interior West stages tantrums called "sagebrush rebellions." It did it against Roosevelt, against Carter, and it is currently amassing shovels in an attempt to get one going against Clinton. At the end of each rebellion, westerners have less power over the federal lands, and less credibility nationally.

Which is too bad, because the vast public lands need the help of on-the-ground westerners. While the federal government can lay down broad guidelines for the land, such as the Endangered Species Act and the Wilderness Act, management can only be done locally. Even if you had a competent and well-armed set of federal land managers, they still would have to live in local communities, send their kids to local schools, and get their hair cut by a local barber. The nation can't occupy the rural West long-term, any more than America was able to occupy Vietnam, or Haiti, or the Panama Canal.

On the other hand, reactionary western leaders who lead campaigns to exterminate wolves in Yellowstone or kill bison in Montana ensure that the rest of America will never feel comfortable loosening its grip on the federal lands.

This age-old game played out again at the ACCESS 2000 conference, but with a new twist from Larry Craig. The senator's core constituency— diehards who still believe that the region will someday exert unilateral control over public lands—was there, but surprisingly, Craig himself was not among them. Instead, he listened attentively to the accounts of consensus efforts among loggers, miners, environmentalists, and federal managers that dominated the conference.

Most of the comments Craig made in response were calming and thoughtful. He spoke against another "sagebrush rebellion." He said westerners don't own the federal trees and grass; and he encouraged those working on consensus to keep up their good work. That was during the day.

At the conference's evening banquet, a different Larry Craig emerged. Reading from a speech written by staff in D.C., he warned against "extreme environmentalists" and their dirty, low-down tricks and their attempts to destroy the West. It was one hell of a speech, and the Wyoming rancher next to me destroyed several tissues sopping up tears streaming down her face.

Which is the real McCoy?—the conciliatory, compromise-seeking Craig or the hell-and-damnation Craig? For the moment, both, as he tests the waters.

If Craig attempts to lead his fellow western senators toward coming to terms with the national desire to protect federal lands, he knows he will be fiercely opposed by some of his present constituency. Some national environmental groups will do what they can to thwart any move toward the center, since the result will be more sovereignty for the West, and less control out of Washington, D.C.

Craig can succeed only if he takes the plunge, and then, as happened with Nixon twenty-eight years ago, a political middle emerges to support him. I think that middle exists, but it lacks a leader. I hope the senator decides to risk his political life to help the West—at long last—grow up.

Utah and the Politics of Acceptance

—Mark Menlove

This Olympics scandal business is complicated. If you believe the Utah politicians and some members of the Salt Lake Olympics Committee, the vote-buying scheme to secure the 2002 Winter Olympics was concocted and carried out entirely by two men: Tom Welch and Dave Johnson. I think there is more to it.

Welch, fallen from grace before the scandal broke, and Johnson, his first lieutenant, certainly fit the image of gift-wielding Rambos whose misguided Olympics zeal led them into a shadowy jungle of incestuous scholarships, gambling junkets, and bogus humanitarian aid. If it is blame we are after, though, perhaps we should look deeper, right down into Utah's cultural roots.

I am not an Olympics insider, but I have been close enough to the Olympics flame to feel its heat and to witness the smoky shadows it casts. During Salt Lake's push to host the 2002 Olympics, I served as president of the Utah Ski Association and its marketing company Ski Utah. Bringing the Olympics to Utah would be good for business, so one of my job responsibilities was to support the bid effort, however possible.

Over the course of four years, the organization I headed contributed several hundred thousand dollars to the Salt Lake Olympics Bid Committee. The ski association's financial support also bought me the privilege of accompanying the bid committee and an entourage of proud and well-to-do Utahns to Budapest in June 1995, where the International Olympics Committee named the host site of the 2002 Games. I can't say that I actually lobbied any IOC members on the trip. The closest I came was waving a flag as the Olympics motorcade drove by.

It was when we were triumphantly greeted back home by thousands of screaming citizens that I felt a sharp cultural edge to the giddy thrill of victory.

For the sake of seeing the culprit more clearly, let me step forward and confess: Like Welch and Johnson, I am a Utah booster, all too eager to show off my home state to the world. Like Welch and Johnson, I grew up in Utah, firmly entrenched in the Mormon culture, the dominant force shaping Utah's collective psyche.

The Mormon pioneers who settled here came to this then isolated and forsaken place because they were different, because the rest of the world did not accept them. Five generations later, the descendants of those pioneers wonder if we are still different. We wonder if we are yet accepted. Our geographic inferiority complex is deep rooted. As Utahns, we are told how odd we are as a people, how peculiar are our liquor laws and our social mores.

It is our neediness, our desperate desire for acceptance, which I believe is at the heart of the scandal. As if taking a cue from our Great Basin topography, Utah and its people are a perfectly prepared petri dish for a culture like Olympics boosterism. What better way to validate ourselves than to invite the world's greatest athletes and brightest spotlights as we host the most coveted sporting event in the universe? I wonder what I, or for that matter any of those other fever-stricken Utahns, would have done in Welch or Johnson's shoes. I want to believe I would have stopped short of handing over a cash-filled envelope to an IOC member, but who knows.

Our Olympics bid proposal touted Utah's striking natural beauty and geographic diversity. Those claims are real. The land is magical, even spiritual. Yet instead of protecting these lands, we Utahns too often devalue our homeland. In the pursuit of popularity, we use the beauty of our state as currency. Here, we seem to say, isn't the place where we live beautiful? Come in, do whatever you want to our beautiful land. The only thing we ask is that you tell us we aren't as strange or peculiar as we fear we are.

Though I recently moved away, my connection to Utah feels stronger than ever. Curiously, my allegiance has grown silent. If you ask me about Utah, I am likely to look away as if I do not hear you. There are some things that are too sacred to be traded away for an elusive fix to a sagging cultural ego. The silence is my penance.

A Land-Based View of Sexual Indiscretion

—Christina Nealson

I don't have to go very far to understand my feelings about President Clinton and the latest sexual scandal—only as far as my old Danish Aunt Clara, a no-nonsense farm woman who survived working forty acres of fenced soil. I can see her now. I walk into her small kitchen that smells of fresh-baked bread and coffee and tell her about the allegations that President Clinton had sexual encounters with Monica Lewinsky.

"Good Lord of Deliverance!" Aunt Clara proclaims. Then she steam-rolls into one of her favorite speeches. A rendition of how men have one master and that's the appendage that hangs between their legs. It ends, as it always does, with "Don't trust men. Just don't trust them."

I smile to myself. (I always smile when Aunt Clara talks this way. I dis-agree with her assessment of men, but then, no man has abandoned me, like her, to raise two boys alone.) When her tirade dies, I tell her about the talk of impeachment, and this tough-love Republican looks at me like I'm crazy. "Is he supposed to tell the world about his sex life? Of course he'll lie. Leave well enough alone. He's doing a good job."

Aunt Clara's response is similar to what I hear from the farm and ranch families of the inner Mountain West, and what the polls confirm. Political correctness be damned. Sexual harassment laws, they believe, are products of a confused, politicized urban woman. These laws fly in the face of biology. They signal a breakdown of community. If someone has a prob-lem with sexual come-ons or attractions, there are other ways to handle it.

Both men and women get caught in their biology. Women get the rap for their monthly chaotic flight of hormones, a time that throws them into periods of profound creativity and intense dreams. A time that is not known for its tactfulness. If we feel it, we say it, and it isn't always nice. Men's testosterone predicament isn't as predictable. Even President Carter admitted to lusting after women.

My farm family didn't talk out loud about this stuff, but we understood it and acted accordingly. The kitchen window offered a ready view of the barnyard, where animals were in constant sexual motion. As for people, monogamy was cherished, but folks weren't naïve. What people that work the land know, what politicians have forgotten, is that you can't legislate morality, just as you can't legislate real power. Real power and autonomy come with the land. That's why my grandfather gave every one of his children, four girls and two boys, forty acres when they left home. That's why Aunt Clara never saw herself as a victim.

My recently published book contains some poetic, erotic passages. One of the most often asked questions at book readings is "Are your parents still alive?" (yes) and "What do they think of these passages?" The answer lies somewhere between Aunt Clara's response and my family's bond with the land. The answer hints at the heartland response to President Clinton's "scandal." "My parents love my book. They are people of the land. The erotic, the sensual, the sexual, is everyday. It's in the fields, a sunset, and one another. And, it's deeply private."

Presidents Washington, Lincoln, Wilson, and Roosevelt had serious sexual relationships outside of their marriages.

Presidents Jefferson, Cleveland, and Harding fathered children out of wedlock.

Presidents Harding, Eisenhower, Kennedy, Johnson, and Clinton had one or more extramarital affairs. And these are the ones we know about.

I don't have to like these escapades to believe that many of these men were good presidents. The world of the sensual is a complicated tar baby—try to explain it and you keep getting caught in your own foreplay of words. What remains strong in my land-based upbringing is the clear message that sexuality does not imply a victim. Like Aunt Clara, I am disappointed in Bill Clinton, but I know what comes with the lay of the land. I voted for Clinton for president. I didn't ask him if he knew how to run fence.

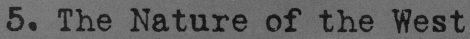

5. The Nature of the West

Enough with the Nature Already
—Stephen Lyons

In a recent column in the on-line magazine *Salon*, Anne Lamott made the following proposal: "Rather than make perfectly good writers crank out new books every few years because they need income and are otherwise unemployable, what if we gave them subsidies not to write any more books, like they give to tobacco growers?"

I would be even more specific: Let's pay "nature writers" not to write any more books for at least ten years. (If Ed Abbey reappears, he gets an exemption.)

This may be heresy, but how many times do we need to wade through some introvert's musings on his or her latest tramp into unspoiled wilderness? Would it hurt anyone to have a moratorium on the word "sacred," or on the following:

"I take a step slowly across the knoll. I listen to coyotes howl. I watch hawks circle on thermals that I feel against my skin, which is attached to my body. If only all of humankind could walk with me and think the same thoughts I have, then all conflicts, cruelty, and madness would cease."(Because I have actually written similar passages, it is only fair that I also abide by the moratorium. Is that applause I hear?)

Recently I gave up trying to read a famous nature writer's latest work after encountering the pronoun "I" eighteen times on the first page. (Fortunately, this was a library book.) The writer appeared lonely, self-centered, and smug all at the same time. He needed friends, a volunteer shift at a soup kitchen in Gallup, or perhaps a year of hard labor in a Montana aluminum smelter.

Along with the moratorium would come new guidelines for writers of nature books. First, the writer would have to participate in cutting down the exact number of trees responsible to produce his or her work. Experienced loggers will offer instruction. After the trees are cut and shipped to the mill, the writer must restore the logged area by sowing native grasses and planting new trees. We'll provide the necessary seed, gloves, and hoedads.

Multicity book tours will also be banned because travel by plane and car contributes to global warming. Newly published authors must limit their reading tours to venues that are within walking distance. This may seem harsh, but all I'm asking is for nature writers to take responsibility for their products.

I truly believe we should love nature, preserve wild places, notice hawks (maybe even magpies and coots), work to curb development and control consumption, and, if possible, grow a beard to convey our woodsman prowess.

But the truth is, most of us in the West live in crowded town-cities, where we are underemployed and overworked. It's rare anymore if we do something as self-indulgent as loading up the fifteen-year-old, oil-dripping rig to drive four hours over crummy washboard roads so we can be alone to write about the experience of being alone. We're more concerned that our knees sound like castanets when we climb stairs; that our children are moving away to cool cities and we aren't; that we need dental work; or that we are not putting enough away for retirement.

Sadly, most Americans don't need wilderness—even though many of them benefit indirectly from such things as pure drinking water originating from high, wilderness drainages. The survival of the lynx or great gray owl is not a national concern despite all the books with the gorgeous covers printed on acid-free, eighty-pound paper cut from national forests.

Amazing as it sounds, I know many wonderful people who live extraordinarily rewarding lives without ever wanting to "experience the silence of the forest" or hear the "haunting cry of the loon." Brooklyn is full of such people. So is France. Yet writers still bombard us with such advice as "Learning to be attentive in the forest opens us up to intimacy and the movement of thought." Don't these books have fact checkers?

Let's expand the literary canon to include loggers, miners, ranchers, Greyhound bus drivers, bored teenagers, Hispanics, Native Americans, and barley farmers. We need books by people who use the land for work and reflection, people who love the earth but have also cut down trees and plowed under sagebrush. Think of the new anthologies: "Women of the West Who Don't Wear Dangling Silver Earrings" or "The Best New Clear-Cut Stories of 1998," edited by Idaho Senator Larry Craig.

"The next ten years will pass quickly and all you nature writers will receive your checks on time at the beginning of each month. In the interim, get out a little bit. Visit a city, take in a baseball game, ride a crowded subway, learn to laugh out loud, and, most of all, try experimenting with the third-person plural pronoun. We'll be in touch."

The Problem with Cows
—*Chris Frasier*

Cows sure are dumb. At least that's what I've been reading lately in the popular press. A man who was convicted this year in Oregon for shooting his neighbor's cows defended himself with the idea that cows aren't smart enough to control their grazing.

As someone who works with cows every day, I'm relieved. I had naïvely seen cattle not as logically challenged but as slow animals prone to follow the herd. Now I see that many of my problems result from their dull thinking.

For example, when I forgot to close a gate and cattle helped themselves to a pasture before it was ready to graze, I used to think it was my fault. Now, thanks to this new insight, I see that it's just those dumb cows. They should understand photosynthesis, the Krebs cycle, and how grass plants store energy. If cows weren't so dense, they could take over many of the management chores that occupy my time. This could give me, and other ranchers, time to pursue new endeavors, like fine arts, perhaps leading to a renaissance of sale-barn ballet.

Another sign that cows show poor judgment is their drinking problem. Of course, this is different from human drinking problems, but then cows aren't intelligent enough to distill and drink addictive substances. No, this has to do with water.

Twice a day, they saunter right up to streams and ponds, put their noses in the water, and drink. Then their instincts take over, their tails go up, and you-know-what comes out. Right into the water. It seems they just can't get over their primordial fear of predators lurking near the water site, so they lighten their load. This hardly creates an atmosphere that makes predators like humans feel welcome.

If cows were more sophisticated, they would do what humans do and pay a dollar a pint for out-of-state water in no-return plastic bottles. You don't see any cow tracks cluttering up the pristine streams shown on those bottles' glossy labels. Which brings up another issue: It's almost impossible to entice cows with slick marketing campaigns.

The problem with cows, it's been said, is that they come from the dumb side of the family. When brains were distributed, their cousin the buffalo (or bison, as they prefer to be called) got a second helping, and cows went away empty. Even Ted Turner, a well-known animal behavior expert, has praised the highly intelligent bison as he fills several western ranches with them.

Everyone knows how intelligent bison are. This fact is well documented by huge piles of bison bones lying at the bottom of twenty-five-foot cliffs. You see, when slow Indians would dress up as even slower dogs and chase a few bison over a creek bank, most of the herd went along dutifully. You see, bison understood the role they played in the colorful history of indigenous peoples and that their deaths meant nothing in contrast to the archaeological legacy they left behind. Cows, in contrast, will hardly be coaxed across a highway for fear of becoming roadkill like so many wild animals.

Speaking of highways, commuting is another intelligent action that cows have failed to learn. While humans long ago realized the benefit of living in one county and working in another, cows continue to live and work in the same place. Since their work consists of grazing, and since grass tends to grow in low areas where the best soil is, some say cattle spend way too much time along creek bottoms.

Building fences or herding them out of these sensitive areas is just too much work for some people, but if cattle would think more like humans, they could solve this problem. By fostering riparian blight and high rates of violent crime, cows would be forced into leaving their work areas as quickly as possible and heading an hour or more into the hills to escape.

The really frustrating thing about cows is the educational opportunities they've wasted. After generations of domestication, you'd think they would have learned a little more from their human caretakers. Apparently, not much has rubbed off during the thousand years of contact with a truly superior creature.

With many of my shortcomings blamed on dumb cattle, I'm feeling much better about myself. It's a shame I hadn't thought of this before. Now, if you'll excuse me, I think there's a gate open somewhere.

The Cow Drive: Better Than TV
—*David Feela*

Western highways have something few other parts of the country can boast. I don't mean mountainous vistas or accessible ski slopes. I mean something most other states have removed from their highways but that we tenaciously cling to: cattle.

Before you get on that proverbial high horse and start snickering, let me explain. You see, I mean, cattle on the highways, not just near them, grazing like a Norman Rockwell picture of ranching life. I mean a herd of 300 or more heading right down the dotted line in spite of those lifetime-guaranteed deer whistles you mounted to your front bumper.

I mean a cattle drive, major cows and cow people carving a cow swath down the middle of a fifty-five-miles-per-hour stretch of country road. I mean full-time cow business, ranchers without semitrailers, steering their livelihood from upper to lower pastures or (depending on the time of year) from lower to upper ones.

If you've been there, you know what I mean. First there's the pickup truck with a red flag—maybe an old pair of flannels—on a stick, waving to catch your attention. Even before that, attentive local drivers will know what's happening if they're coming up from the rear end of the event. Drivers in Denver, Albuquerque, and Salt Lake City understand the term "brown out" in a slightly different context than we cattle country people do. Once these indicators clearly mark the road, there's no avoiding the inevitable. Really, other than those desperate people with appointments to keep who aren't smart enough to own a cellular phone, who would want to?

There's no feeling so close to nature as having your car engulfed and buffeted by a stream of live beef. If you keep the windows closed, your children will hang from the glass like fruit bats, eyes wide, wild with the excitement of the in-your-face experience. It's reality without an ounce of virtual. I've seen children on the curb waving as if they were watching a parade, each horse and rider a celebrity, each cow a moving wonder.

The real interest for me has been in watching the drivers' faces as they creep by, for creep they must. Each vehicle becomes just another part of the herd, a techno-cow if you will, joining the slow-motion migration. Some expressions behind those windshields are frustrated, spitting inaudible curses against the glass. Others look away nervously, casting cow-to-cow glances as 1,150 pounds polish a driver's side-door handle.

Once I watched a driver literally shrink out of sight as an excited animal attempted to mount a less willing mate. I could see the image forming in the driver's head, both animals coming down on her thin metal hood as if it were a cheap motel mattress. Or the rearview mirror glance, all the time suspecting that cattle have no clear preference in their tiny brains for the anatomical differences between themselves and a Ford Taurus. Drivers obliged to adapt themselves to a pace of life that registers below the increments of cruise control express a kaleidoscope of emotion.

Another thing a cattle drive brings out, besides the obvious glimpse of time-held traditions in ranching, is our fastidious taste for cleanliness. My native Minnesotan father, after driving his RV through his first cattle drive in Colorado, rushed to my house and turned on the garden hose so he could wash the pie from his chrome plate. It's a fact: Cows drool. They slobber, they poop, they sweat and moo. They bellow out of their confusion and long for the quiet of a mountain pasture, away from the jerky ways of human beings. Indeed, they should. Cows historically haven't fared well in the contest for the survival of the fastest.

There's a stampede of opinion about how American ranching should keep up with technology; this is where I'll gladly step aside. And not because I don't care. It's just not my spread, not my expertise. But avoid a cattle drive? Not a chance!

L.A. continues to stack its freeways and New York digs its subways. If the information highway is going to run right through my living room, moving cattle on-line would seem to be the next logical step. Thank goodness logic has its limits.

Wily Coyote
—*Dan Whipple*

The coyote, wrote Mark Twain, "is a living, breathing allegory of Want. He is always hungry. He is always poor, out of luck and friendless. The meanest creatures despise him, and even the fleas would desert him for a velocipede."

This description has held up pretty well in the 140 years since Twain crossed the Rockies in a stagecoach. Always the underdog, the coyote provokes howls of protest from western sheepmen and the owners of small pets that the opportunistic predators haul off—but nothing has been able to stop the irrepressible coyote.

Not even the federal government, which under its gently named Wildlife Services Agency—formerly Animal Damage Control—has killed an average of 100,000 coyotes a year since 1990. Coyotes kill sheep at the rate of about a quarter of a million annually. Unlike the government, they do not charge the taxpayer for this service.

The feds and the ranchers they support don't give up easily. Several are bringing back a failed method for stopping coyote predation on sheep— the deadly Compound 1080. In yet another creative use for Velcro, ranchers will hang toxic collars around the necks of their sheep in the hope that hungry coyotes will bite their prey there and die—a pretty high price to pay for a meal.

The 1080 collars are approved for use in Montana, South Dakota, Wyoming, Texas, and New Mexico. Oregon, Utah, Ohio, and West Virginia have also recently applied for approval.

Sheep industry legend has it that the golden age of predator control was between 1950 and 1972, when coyotes could legally be poisoned with Compound 1080. Poisoned-bait carcasses were laid hither and thither, killing coyotes, along with the inevitable collateral damage to nontarget species that fed on carrion—eagles, crows, domestic dogs, and so on.

President Richard Nixon banned 1080 in 1972, and ever since then the industry has blamed its sheep losses in part on that ban. There's only one problem: They're wrong.

According to a landmark study by Utah State University's Frederic Wagner, from the time 1080 was introduced in 1950, lamb losses from predation actually increased over the entire twenty-two years that 1080 was used. Predation began to decline only in 1975—three years after 1080 was banned. One explanation for this bewildering trend is that the coyotes got smart and simply stopped eating any animals that they hadn't killed themselves.

Far from laying Compound 1080 in its well-deserved grave, ranching interests search for ever more efficient ways to get around the ban. Enter the toxic collar.

It won't work either. Coyotes, unlike federal agencies, learn from experience. The University of Colorado's Marc Bekoff, the world's leading authority on coyote behavior, says, "My guess is that they will avoid sheep with collars, and the others will learn by observation."

The coyote is the only large predator in the United States that has increased its U.S. range, boldly going where no coyote has gone before—New England, Arkansas, even Central Park in New York City. Once confined west of the Mississippi River, *Canis latrans* has gone national, opening franchises in New England, which never had coyotes at all until the last couple of decades. Florida has some coyotes that eat turtle eggs. In Arkansas, coyotes mangle watermelons to the extent that the agriculture department writes reports about it.

A coyote will eat nearly anything. In a 1938 Yellowstone study, biologist Adolph Murie found quite an assortment in coyotes' diets: paper, canvas and leather gloves, a butter wrapper, twine, leather (one piece containing a rivet), cellophane, eight inches of rope, isinglass, three square inches of towel, a match, a mouse nest, and seven inches of curtain. In Murie's study, a coyote was more likely to have eaten a canvas or leather glove than a mushroom.

All of this luxurious dining has continued in spite of the concerted effort of the federal government to prevent it.

There are other ways to stop coyote predation on sheep. Ranchers who clean up the carcasses of sheep that die on the range have almost no coyote predation problems. Then there is another method that simply calls for bringing back the coyote's chief ecological competitor, the wolf. You could reduce coyote predation by reintroducing the wolf, as has been shown in

Yellowstone's National Park, where recently introduced wolves have killed coyotes.

This might have the side benefit of reducing the number of sheep even more. Now there's an idea we can all get behind.

Babysitting Salmon

—*John Rosapepe*

Sixteen years ago I was a baby-sitter for the Army Corps of Engineers. Wearing a hard hat and steel-toed boots, I tended salmon and steelhead young on their 300-mile barge trip down the lower Snake and Columbia Rivers.

We barged the fish because the rivers where salmon and steelhead had evolved over thousands of years were no longer friendly to them. Salmon runs in Idaho declined precipitously after eight dams were built on the lower reaches of the Snake and Columbia Rivers. Migrating juvenile salmon faced a lethal mix of slow-moving reservoirs filled with unseasonably warm water and deadly hydropower turbine blades. What once had been a seven- to ten-day trip to the ocean for the fish had turned into a forty-day nightmare.

The Corps had a technological fix: If salmon and steelhead couldn't adapt to the dams, the solution was to take them out of the river and transport them through and around the dams on barges or trucks. I was an eager recruit at the time, caught up in the belief that we didn't have to choose between salmon and dams.

We began collecting fish at Lower Granite Dam, surrounded by the rolling wheat fields of southeast Washington. About half of the salmon and steelhead were diverted away from the turbine portals and spillways through a series of Rube Goldberg devices and transported down tubes for a quarter mile below the dam. There they were shunted to holding raceways and pumped into tanks on awaiting barges.

Fish biologists from Idaho, Washington, and Oregon's Department of Fish and Wildlife eagerly cycled through Lower Granite Dam to see how we were saving the fish from extinction. Our distinctive red barges sported large signs letting the public know that the Corps was doing its part to save salmon through its Operation Fish Run. I monitored the fish every four hours on the day-and-a-half trip down the rivers, maintaining the right mixture of oxygen and temperature of the water in the holds by running it through aerators mounted on the barge.

After the 100-degree heat of eastern Washington, it was always a relief to come into the verdant and cool Columbia Gorge with its cascading waterfalls. If we were lucky, the setting sun would illuminate Mount Hood's snowcapped peak in hues of purple and orange.

When it came time to release the fish, I would say a prayer for their safe return from the ocean in a few years. Unfortunately, neither my prayers nor the barging has worked. Salmon and steelhead numbers have continued to decline since barging began and the returns for the barged salmon are no better than for fish that remained in the river and ran the dams. Perhaps the barged salmon fail to glean some critical homing cues that are only found in the river. Maybe the stress of being moved into the unnatural conditions of a barge is too much, but now it's obvious: Packing wild fish in metal cans didn't work then, and it doesn't work now.

Idaho coho salmon have since gone extinct and sockeye salmon have all but disappeared. Adult runs of 75,000 wild Chinook salmon that were common in the 1960s have dwindled to a few thousand these days. Wild steelhead runs have fared no better. Steelhead and salmon runs on the Clearwater and Salmon Rivers that Lewis and Clark wrote about are now destined to become mere footnotes in our history books.

So why are we holding so tightly to the failed barging experiment? I ask that question every spring and summer as the fish barges make the same downriver journey I did sixteen years ago. I wonder what the new salmon baby-sitters think. Is it just a paycheck for them or are they kidding themselves—as I did—that they are making a difference?

Admitting that human technology can't replace natural processes is hard for our society, especially when it would mean undoing monuments built in the name of progress. Getting rid of the dams on the lower Snake River, however, offers the only chance we have to bring back the salmon. Our rivers need to be turned back into rivers. They need to flow unimpeded as they did for thousands of generations as the salmon evolved a way of life seemlessly intertwined with the currents.

Grizzlies and the Male Animal
—*Louise Wagenknecht*

The crowd of several hundred area residents who gathered recently in a school auditorium in Salmon, Idaho, was almost totally united in its opposition to the proposal. No one wanted the U.S. Fish and Wildlife Service to introduce some twenty-five subadult grizzly bears into the Selway–Bitterroot Wilderness on the Idaho–Montana border over a period of several years.

During the four-hour hearing, speaker after speaker rose to denounce grizzlies, in any place, in any form. Most dwelt at length on their bloodthirstiness. A few speakers mentioned questions about available food resources, effects on salmon and steelhead, and possible restrictions on the livestock, timber, and recreational industries, but these were overshadowed by the general angst.

Big, stout, fully grown men displayed the kind of hostility and fear bordering on panic that, when voiced by women, is usually dismissed as hysteria. Their terror was evoked by the mere possibility that something bigger, stronger, faster, and at least as aggressive as they might again roam the vast wildernesses of central Idaho and western Montana. My husband was especially amused to see that this fear was most often couched in terms of concern for wives and children and aged parents by men who never, under any circumstances, allow their wives to accompany them and their male friends into the mountains during elk season.

They viewed with horror the possible presence of a creature so large and powerful, so subject to quick and sometimes violent turns of mood, at large within the Selway–Bitterroot, and someday, perhaps, within Idaho's Frank Church–River of No Return and Gospel Hump Wildernesses.

Welcome to the real world, guys.

Welcome to what women face every day of every year of our lives: close encounters with unpredictable creatures subject to violent bursts of adrenaline-driven rage. Creatures faster, stronger, and more aggressive than we; creatures because of whom we lock our doors, load our guns, and avoid dark streets. Even those specimens with inoffensive temperaments sometimes take to the public highways after ingesting mind-altering, inhibition-reducing chemicals, under the quaint impression that they are actually in control of the 4,000 pounds of hurtling metal and rubber under their feet.

Our news sources are largely devoted to regular accounts of the accidents, homicides, assaults, and other mayhem perpetrated by these creatures, usually affecting the females and young of my species, which is also, alas, theirs.

Yet many local representatives of this perilous breed are completely unmanned at the prospect of sharing a portion of the northern Rockies with grizzly bears. At the Salmon hearing, they scoffed loudly at suggestions that clean camping and other simple precautions go far toward eliminating dangerous encounters in grizzly country. Real men, I guess, don't use pepper spray or put their food in bearproof containers. They carry guns and scorn keeping a low profile.

Cougars have been found under porches only a few miles from town, and a few years ago one ate five of our sheep. Black bears, which have killed as many people as have grizzlies in the United States, roam right up to the city limits of Salmon, but they and cougars are big game animals in Idaho, and their pursuit with hounds a much enjoyed sport. Some hound men don't even kill their quarry, merely subjecting it, once treed, to a paparazzi-like barrage of photos before leashing the hounds and going home.

Black bears and cougars are part of the culture of the country. No one calls for their extermination, no matter how many kids they eat on Indian reservations in Montana or in the public parks of California.

Most of the anti-grizzly speakers also support the continued operation of the Salmon area's largest single business enterprise, an open-pit gold mine that last year led the nation in bullion production. Yet again and again I hear longtime Lemhi County residents lament the increase in local crime since the mine, with its hundreds of employees, came to a county that had not experienced a murder in decades.

We are getting used to killings now, and to burglaries, assaults, vandalism, and drug stings. So I wonder, which is more dangerous, grizzlies or strangers of our own species, welcomed here without question by a philosophy of free enterprise at any price?

Vermin to Vermin
—*Mark Matthews*

The man in the lobby of the motel looks like a nice guy. He's clean-cut, in his late sixties, polite, and gregarious. Yet, even though I smile back at him, I don't dare talk to him. He is a prairie-dog shooter.

I'm usually pretty open-minded when it comes to people's points of view. I can sympathize with strip miners, drink a beer with loggers, joke with Earth First!ers, but I find it hard to fraternize with someone who gets a kick out of pinging the heads off prairie dogs.

Bad news is it's a growing sport.

At Thunder Basin National Grasslands in Wyoming, sportsmen report shooting anywhere from 250 to 1,000 animals per day. On the Fort Belknap Indian Reservation in Montana, shooters cull about 35 percent of the prairie-dog population every year. At South Dakota's Conata Basin, which borders Badlands National Park, officials report up to 4,000 shooter days per year.

It seems other people also want the carnage stopped. The majority of comments on a recent draft environmental assessment for national grasslands on the Great Plains want to see more conservation of prairie dogs rather than control and eradication.

We're not talking hunting rights here. This is nothing more than target practice. Prairie-dog shooters leave the carcasses where they fall. I probably wouldn't mind so much if they skinned the animals and then made a fricassee out of them like some families on the Fort Belknap Indian Reservation do. But most prairie-dog hunters seem to care only about statistics: how many they shot in a week, day, hour, or from what distance they knocked the rodents' heads off.

Mention prairie-dog shooting to real hunters and they'll either roll their eyes or say outright it's the most ridiculous thing they've ever heard of. Real hunters, you see, respect wildlife.

I'll give the sharpshooters the benefit of the doubt, though. Maybe they indulge in their sport out of ignorance. They could still be under the impression that the prairie dog is the scourge of the prairie, that it eats up grass faster than a vacuum cleaner sucks dog hairs off a rug.

Blame the bum rap on two ecologists who, in 1924, published their accounts of prairie dogs in the *U.S. Agricultural Bulletin*. W. P. Taylor and J.V.G. Loftfield described the prairie dog as "one of the most injurious rodents of the Southwest and plains regions" because it removed "vegetation in its entirety from the vicinity of its home."

That report fueled a wave of eradication programs that poisoned 20 million acres of prairie-dog towns. Today, 99 percent of the historic prairie-dog population, estimated at 5 billion, is gone. The original habitat of the species is thought to have covered 98 million acres—an area larger than Montana.

Now some ecologists say the prairie dog actually enhances the range. Craig Knowles, a leading expert on prairie ecology, told me prairie-dog towns are full of plant life, even though they appear desolate. "The animal's digging activity disturbs the soil, and weedy plants take over, much like in a cultivated field. When closely cropped, these plants become higher in protein and nitrogen content and are sought out by cattle, bison, antelope, and elk."

Of more importance, the prairie dog is a keystone species, creating a unique ecosystem on which many other animals depend. Take away prairie-dog towns and you may also be signing the death certificates of the black-footed ferret, swift fox, ferruginous hawk, mountain plover, burrowing owl, and golden eagle, among others. So many animals eat prairie dogs that early ecologists dubbed the dog towns the prairie's grocery stores.

It doesn't help that flea-borne sylvatic plague recently wiped out many dog towns across the West. Montana has only half the prairie-dog acreage it had a dozen years ago. Yet the shooting continues, with federal land management agencies distributing maps showing locations of prairie dog towns to shooters.

In some cases, the target practice is jeopardizing the black-footed ferret recovery program. The ferret has been on the endangered species list for thirty years but so far has been reintroduced at only four sites, with two other locations being considered. To be delisted ten sites in all are needed, but some land mangers are working harder to contain prairie-dog numbers than enhance them, so there are no other potential sites.

It's time to quit using an old excuse to slaughter this important animal. If we are really committed to restoring our native habitats, we must start with this lowly rodent.

Prairie Dogs Unlimited
—*Ed Quillen*

When I was in junior high school, I got my first memorable exposure to the mixed blessings of progress. On many occasions before that sad day, I pedaled my clunky old bicycle to a prairie-dog town on the outskirts of Greeley, on the Great Plains of northern Colorado.

I could coast in quietly and watch the rodents go about their business until a sentinel noticed me and yelped. Then they'd all run down their burrows and hide for a few minutes, before returning, one by one, to the surface—as long as I stayed still.

One spring day. I found transits and stakes, along with an active bulldozer, instead of prairie dogs. The sign said a new junior high school was under construction. How could they destroy an educational prairie-dog town just to build a torture chamber designed to imprison, stifle, and bore teenaged boys like me?

My parents offered consolation. Even if that colony were gone forever, there were zillions of other prairie dogs spread across the vast Great Plains.

They were right, but that was thirty-five years ago. Now the U.S. Fish and Wildlife Service is considering the black-tailed prairie dog for listing under the Endangered Species Act. There may have once been 1.5 billion of them spread across 250 million acres, but thanks to new schools—and highways, subdivisions, shopping malls, and intensive agriculture—habitat is now down to 700,000 acres.

Prairie dogs aren't really dogs. They're football-sized vegetarian rodents with short legs and tails. They got the name because their calls sound like barks. They dig tunnels on the prairie and live in towns with thousands of residents. There are five species in North America. Two are thriving—the white-tailed and the Gunnison—but the Utah is threatened, and the Mexican endangered, and now the black-tailed is in trouble, too.

Prairie dogs convert grass, indigestible by many animals, into edible protein, which makes them the base of the food chain for hawks, ferrets, and bobcats. Their burrows provide housing for snakes and burrowing owls.

Many ranchers see them as the enemy. The "varmints" eat forage that is supposed to go to cattle, and their holes break the legs of human and beast. Ranchers respond with guns, traps, and poison.

Even though some ranchers are prominent supporters of the "property rights movement," they've lost their moral compass on the prairie-dog issue, as recent action in the Colorado legislature demonstrates.

An environmental group, the Boulder-based Southern Plains Land Trust, recently bought 1,200 acres in Baca County (the part of Colorado closest to Oklahoma) for a preserve for relocated prairie dogs in the path of Front Range development—a model private conservation initiative if there ever was one. But did the cattlemen say, "We want other people to respect our property rights, so we respect the environmentalists' right to do what they want with their land, even if we don't exactly approve?" Of course not. They lobbied the state legislature for a law that forbids importing "destructive rodent pests" without consent of the affected county commissioners.

To their credit, some conservative Republicans opposed this as an assault on private property rights, but at last report, the law was on its way to the governor's desk. This seems sad—you can import all the cows you want to your property, but you can't bring in prairie dogs, which were around long before the cow and horse arrived.

Is there a solution?

Consider the success of such organizations as Ducks Unlimited and Trout Unlimited. They kill animals, but they want the fish and fowl to flourish, and so the members work effectively for habitat preservation and enhancement.

A friend who hunts prairie dogs (the thriving Gunnison) tells me that the national Varmint Hunters Association has 40,000 members and that some outfitters get $350 a day to conduct prairie-dog hunts. Note also that the Southern Plains Land Trust was able to raise $198,000 to buy the Baca County land for proposed prairie-dog habitat. This means that the resources are present, if organized properly, for a powerful new conservation group: Prairie Dogs Unlimited.

The varmint hunters, various environmental organizations, and many of us plain citizens do share a goal—more habitat and thus more prairie dogs for a healthy Great Plains, just as Ducks Unlimited wants more marshes for more duck habitat and thereby more ducks to hunt.

People for the Ethical Treatment of Animals wouldn't like it—a bunch of guys squinting through their rifle scopes to blast furry little animals. Yet name one piece of habitat that PETA has ever protected and then look at the solid accomplishments of the trout takers and duck killers. There's every reason to believe the varmint hunters would be just as effective.

Can the environmental movement even consider making such an alliance for the good of the Great Plains ecosystem? Or is it as short-sighted as the property-rights movement?

The Wolf and the Rancher
—Michael J. Robinson

The recent spate of violence directed at the most endangered subspecies of wolf in the world should teach us the folly of trying to compromise with extremists.

In the first few months after the reintroduction of the Mexican gray wolf into the wilds of southeastern Arizona, five animals have been shot, and two more are missing from among the original eleven released in a reintroduction program and the one pup subsequently born in the wild. The remaining animals have been recaptured.

Interior Secretary Bruce Babbitt has condemned the shootings and vowed to leave no stone unturned to catch the malefactors. More importantly, he has pledged to persevere in the reintroduction effort.

However, his actions belie his own words. Babbitt knows who the first shooter is: Richard Humphry, who first claimed a wolf was attacking his dog, then, upon learning that would not suffice to exonerate him, claimed the wolf was running toward his wife.

A necropsy on the wolf revealed it was standing, not running, when shot broadside. Humphry was never charged and was subsequently feted as the keynote speaker in a Catron County, New Mexico, anti-environmental get-together this summer. Catron County is part of the wolf recovery zone just over the state line and is famous for its militias and challenges to constitutional government.

If Babbitt's mistake were limited to deciding not to prosecute Humphry, he could perhaps be excused. Yet he structured the entire reintroduction effort around placating a small minority: ranchers, whose leadership has never respected the right of all Americans to participate in decisions on wildlife and public lands.

The ranchers of Catron County do not represent many of the people who live there. According to a League of Women Voters survey, 52 percent of residents of rural southwestern New Mexico (Catron, Grant, Sierra, and Otero Counties) support wolf reintroduction, and only 34 percent oppose it.

Still, ranchers dominate the region's politics, and the ranching mind-set has long manifested in Catron County's signature statutes, such as the one setting jail terms for Forest Service officials who reduce grazing on public lands, or the version of a bounty for coyotes, in which several of the unlucky canids are captured, inconspicuously ear tagged and released, with up to a thousand dollars allocated to anyone subsequently turning in one of the tags.

While certainly distasteful, there is nothing unconstitutional about a bounty on coyotes, but local ranchers go much further. On a bright winter morning six years ago, I listened for hours as one of the county's ad hoc advisors, his legal acumen only matched by his formidable avoirdupois, explained to me that federal taxes were unconstitutional and that New Mexico was the highest duly constituted government authority in the region. The federal government, he said, was a legal fiction.

His background was typical of many of those claiming an ancient "custom and culture" to justify special prerogatives: After abandoning a mining venture on a Caribbean island he had moved to Catron County, bought a ranch, and started selling real estate. What, I asked him as the morning turned into late afternoon, would Catron County's finest do if they lost their court cases? We're armed, he explained to me, and getting ready to fight the feds.

With this truculent political tone in mind, Babbitt decided protecting the wolves could best be accomplished by agreeing to every single ranching demand. He allowed ranchers to kill wolves that kill cattle under some circumstances (no cattle have been killed so far); he limited the recovery area to the boundaries of the Blue Range and the Gila National Forest (ignoring wolf habitat on adjoining public land); and he refused to designate critical habitat where the wolves' survival would be prioritized over extractive land uses. As a result of this latter provision, there are no limits on public-land grazing, or road closures to protect the wolves. At least some of these wolves were probably shot by someone leaning out of a pickup truck.

It is time to admit that the conciliatory approach has failed and begin protecting the wolves' habitat and securing their safety. Roads should be closed around the wolves, grazing allotments terminated, and the animals placed directly in the Gila Wilderness where access is much more difficult.

Instead, Babbitt suggests tax breaks for ranchers to encourage them to support wolves—a gratuitous subsidy for an industry that already enjoys millions of dollars in tax breaks and a smorgasbord of federal services— but still won't abide by the law.

What's the next step for our innovative Secretary of Interior? A federal bounty on the wolves to ensure their popularity? The politics of ranching will apparently make anything seem reasonable.

Living with the Big Bad Wolf
—*Tom Reed*

A decade ago, a friend and I entered a store in a small southwestern New Mexico town. Behind the counter, a red-faced man with a broad-brimmed hat thought he recognized kindred spirits, men of the same mold. We were dusty and red-faced and wore broad-brimmed hats as well.

For the past week, we had been scrambling and sweating up steep canyons and down shaded draws in search of Coues white-tailed deer and Mearns quail. The store was a resupply, a brief touch with civilization before our return to granite, oak, and cactus.

"Here, you folks need to sign this to stop them from bringing back the wolf," he said, shoving a clipboard across the counter at us.

My friend, a soft-spoken, gray-haired retired game warden gently, firmly, pushed the petition back. Unsigned. "You're probably looking at a couple of fellas who would like to see the wolf back."

Spluttering, amazed. "Why, them damn wolves will eat fifteen pounds of red meat in a day! They want to spend 10 million dollars of our money to bring them back. They'll wipe us out!"

I thought back to a sheltered draw that I had worked only a day before. Hoping to flush out a beautiful white-tailed buck, I bumped a Brahman steer out of its bed. It crashed through the brush stupidly, then stopped to stare at me before trotting on, waving good-bye with its manure-smeared rump. There's some red meat that I'd gladly give a wolf, I thought. If he'd eat it.

We paid for our supplies and left the man to stew and fret about his cows. Tolerance doesn't come easy.

In 1942, a wolf family was found at Fort Huachuca in southern Arizona. The family was bothering no one for there were no livestock on the military installation. White-tailed deer, the most common prey of the Mexican gray wolf, were abundant, but the wolves could not be tolerated. A trapper with the Predatory Animal and Rodent Control Service was brought in. He trapped the male and found the den of young pups, which he dispatched efficiently. The female escaped, though, probably into Mexico where she likely met a similar fate.

In the mid-1970s, tracks of a lone wolf were discovered west of Sulphur Springs Valley in southeastern Arizona. The wolf, an apparent wandering male from Mexico, was dubbed the Aravaipa wolf and subsequently exterminated. The ultimate predator—man—had proven his prowess once again.

The history books read the same in every state in the West, from Wyoming to New Mexico, Montana to Colorado. Save for a few remnant pockets, the wolf has been wiped out everywhere. Wolves, indeed, will never wipe us out. We don't have a thing to fear from wolves. It's the other way around.

In the West, no one can remember what it was like living when wolves posed an actual, true threat to the livelihoods of ranchers. One hundred years ago, the wolf was on its way out. In this century, the wolf in the West has been a casual migrant. Never in the past hundred years has the wolf threatened the very survival of humans, any human.

The sad fact is that we seldom have made an attempt to get along with wolves. By and large, wolves have been taboo, especially in the West. We poisoned and trapped them when they no longer posed a threat to our economy. We shot and exterminated the last few until there were no more.

One hundred years ago, the wolf was staggering toward extinction. Gone was its prey base of buffalo, antelope, deer, and elk. New, slower, weaker animals had entered the wolf's territory. Naturally, wolves turned to cattle and sheep to stay alive. Naturally, men turned against wolves to save their stock.

Today, the antelope are back, the deer are flourishing, the elk are abundant, and even the bison have returned in some places. People are also flourishing. Livestock numbers, though, have been trimmed from the masses of animals that pulverized and overgrazed the West at the turn of the century. Reality, it seems, is the final judge of what the range can support. The wolf, though, is generally still missing from the big picture.

In Yellowstone, we're battling the wolf once again—more correctly, battling over the wolf. Judges and courts will decide if the wolf stays, not guns and traps. In the desert Southwest, we're poised to bring back another "experimental" population of wolves. Will we learn from our mistakes of the distant and not-distant past?

We have proven that we can live without wolves. Now it's time to prove that we can live with them. Intolerance is easy. It's tolerance that's a challenge.

Killing the Snake in the Grass
—Hal Walter

The big snake coiled and commenced to rattle its tail when I was still about ten yards away. It had been sunning in the barrow ditch. When I approached on my morning jog, it had done what all good rattlers do and warned me of its presence.

I made sure where my dog was, then slowly walked up and looked at the buzzworm, coiled and menacing, its body as thick as my wrist, its wedge-shaped head up and alert. My neighbor, I could see from here, was preparing for a horseback ride. I knew that her route would take her past the snake. Figuring I could help prevent a spooked horse and a possible wreck, I jogged home and called to warn her of the snake in the ditch.

"Hal, that snake needs to be killed," she answered quickly. After all, we all have animals—horses, dogs, burros—and that snake is a threat to them. If I wouldn't kill the snake, she'd have to call another neighbor and get him to do it.

The pressure was on.

I hoped the snake would be long gone as I put my shotgun in the truck and drove up to check it out. To my surprise and dismay, the snake had uncoiled and was stretched out magnificently in the ditch. I looked it over, all several feet of it, and decided right then that there was no way I could kill this rattler. I tossed some rocks in its direction, hoping to scare it off, but it didn't even coil.

I got back in the truck and drove up to the neighbor's house. "I cannot in good conscience kill that snake," I told her.

"Oh, Hal, that snake has to go," the neighbor shrieked, shaking her head. "It's going to bite one of our animals."

I told her that if the snake was in my corral or against my house that it would be a different story, but it was just out along the road minding its own business. Besides, the snake had warned me at a good distance. I told her that if that snake doesn't bite one of her animals, the next one will. You can't eradicate them.

I drove off, and when I passed the place in the ditch where the snake had been lying, I noticed that it was now gone.

I recalled running down a trail a few years ago and seeing a snake only as my foot came down on its tail. I felt the buzz underfoot. Since I was running, my foot was back in the air by the time the snake rolled over to strike. I received two perfect puncture wounds in the forefoot of my shoe. By the time I had figured out that only my shoe had been poisoned, the rattler was slithering off through the bushes.

An older fellow showed up at my door once and told me that as a boy he had lived in the tiny line shack near my house. Among his other stories, the most captivating was the one he told about the rattlesnake den he and his father found one autumn in the rock pile behind my place. They stuck a pitchfork inside and the snakes coiled around the tines, forming a ball of buzzworms. It took the strength of both of them to lift it out. They shot many of the snakes with a .22 as they slithered away, but there were still more down the hole. They ended up dowsing the den with gasoline and setting it afire.

It's a strange policy we have here in the West, to kill rattlesnakes on sight, when fewer people die of snakebites than of hantavirus, a pestilence spread largely by deer mice, a chief food of rattlesnakes. Yet it doesn't seem the mass-eradication effort has had any long-lasting effect. There's still a good number of snakes around here.

Settlers moving here in earlier days were able to successfully eradicate some species that made this a less-than-comfortable place to live—most notably grizzly bears and wolves—but rattlesnakes have managed to survive. One can only guess that their mostly nocturnal and elusive nature and the average yearly production of up to twelve snakelets per mama rattler have maintained the population.

Later that day, I drove past the place where the snake had buzzed at me that morning. On the opposite side of the road it lay dead. Someone had come along and done what I wouldn't do. It seemed a shame the snake had died for no decent reason. Hopefully, there will always be lots of rattlers where that one came from.

The High Cost of Roadkill

—Mark Matthews

The big buck suddenly appears in my headlights like a statue standing in the middle of the two-lane highway. I brake, swerve to the right, trying not to go off the road. I think I'm past the deer, then it lowers its head and seems to ram into my right fender on purpose, as if it were fending off a competing stag.

The headlight goes black, I hear the thump of metal on soft flesh, the animal's face rakes past the side window. My stomach sinks to my feet. I've killed another animal.

Although I don't have an "I Brake for Animals" bumper sticker, I am a very cautious and defensive driver. I slow down in the evening and on curves. I keep a sharp eye on the roadside ahead. Still, I've hit three deer in the last five years. I suppose I would have gotten rid of my battered truck by now if I hadn't rebuilt the engine just before hitting my second victim. Now the bodywork bill is way beyond my means and no one would buy it.

Practically no driver is innocent of highway carnage. In fact, we've killed so many animals and seen so many carcasses by the roadside that we've grown insensitive to it. "Sleeping deer, sleeping dog, sleeping bear," is what we tell young children. "There's plenty more in the woods. Don't worry."

However, that may not be the case for some animals. Many researchers have studied the effects of dirt roads on wildlife populations in remote areas, but few have looked into the effects of paved highways. The few that have offer some startling insight.

Since 1981, 65 percent of endangered Florida panther deaths have been attributed to vehicle collisions. Cars and trucks in Texas have taken a toll on the endangered ocelot, reducing the population to about eighty animals. In one year near Banff National Park in Alberta, seven gray wolves were killed by vehicles, two by trains. That equaled that year's litters of pups.

In upstate New York, at a Canadian lynx reintroduction site, seventeen of thirty-eight radio-collared animals were killed in traffic collisions. In Florida, where traffic on some roads increased 100 percent in recent years, the collision-caused mortality for black bears increased 1,800 percent.

Not only large mammals are affected. Near the Ninepipes Reservoir in Montana, drivers smash hundreds of painted turtles each summer on Highway 93. The same thing happens to salamanders in Massachusetts, endangered toads near Houston, and endangered desert tortoises in California.

Also in the Gold Rush State, many barn owls are struck and killed as they scout roadsides at night for mice. Even migrating fish such as bull trout and salmon are affected when they cannot negotiate poorly designed culverts under roads. That doesn't take into account the millions of deer, elk, moose, squirrels, raccoons, rabbits, birds, and other common animals that die on the roads each year.

Historically, the federal highway system has received exemptions from the environmental process because of its early relationship to national defense. Now, more than 2 percent of the Lower 48 is covered by roads and their roadsides. That's as much territory as within the state of Georgia.

The ecological impacts of roads significantly affect a much larger area, researchers say. Noise, water pollution, habitat fragmentation, and exhaust emissions are some of the far-reaching by-products of roads and traffic that may kill or keep certain species of animals out of an area.

There is some good news though. Engineers finally are beginning to take wildlife into account as they plan roads. Congress even approved some funding for wildlife mitigation projects in the $198 billion Transportation Equity Act for the 21st Century. There is potentially $3 billion available for wildlife mitigation. The money must be shared with at least nine other programs, including such projects as preserving historic trans-portation structures, getting rid of billboards, and converting abandoned rail lines to trails.

Structures such as wildlife underpasses and overpasses have proven suc-cessful in Europe and Canada. Florida panthers are faring much better since twenty-four underpasses were constructed along Alligator Alley north of Everglades National Park.

Still, environmentalists must be sharp if our society is to finally reduce animal carnage along roads. They must identify key wildlife cor-ridors and make sure engineers install some type of safe passage for animals during the multibillion-dollar construction projects aimed at rebuilding roads across the West in the next decade.

It won't be money wasted on animals. Ask anyone who has totaled their vehicle or sustained an injury in a crash with a moose, elk, or grizzly bear.

Hart and Soul
—*David Peterson*

Each September, after hunting for as long as a month, finally, at some perfectly unpredictable moment an animal appears—intimately close, inexplicably insouciant. At times like this, it's understandable that traditional hunting peoples around the globe were and are adamant that animals sometimes "give themselves" to hunters—at least to those whose hearts are good. As Leslie Marmon Silko sings in her transfigurative "Deer Song":

> I will go with you
> because you love me
> while I die.

Here before me now stands the bull. Suddenly, all the weeks of sleep I've happily missed, all the miles hiked and mountains climbed, the rain and hail and cold endured, merge toward a denouement.

Reenacting the essential drama of human history, my universe shrinks to a single hair on the auburn chest. Arm and shoulder muscles flex, bending the bow. When all feels right, fingers relax and arrow leaps away.

The elk, unaware of its carefully concealed predator, reacts as if it had been stung by a wasp, wheeling and running a few steps—then stops and gazes calmly about, flicking its ears at flies. Does it even know?

"Please," I whisper, "die fast." As if granting my plea, the young bull sways, stumbles, and falls. Soon comes the release of a final breath—breath, anima, soul, spirit leaping away from flesh.

Easing close, I touch the animal with my bow—it doesn't react—then fall to my knees and peer into those dark, inscrutable eyes. In those mirrored orbs is reflected my own fragility, my own ephemeral mortality. To fail to feel the unity this implies, one would have to be spiritually numb. This is a sacred moment.

Suddenly, from out in the silent woods and not so far away, rings one brassy bugle, followed by the sharp crackling of heavy hooves crushing brittle downfall and a bemused chorus of birdlike cow and calf chirps. Life flows on. The cows among that little herd are already pregnant, or soon will be. If the Colorado mountain winter is hard, there'll be one less mouth competing for increasingly scarce browse.

Down in the valleys, where the highways bristle with an unending flood tide of urban refugees, are some who would condemn "my kind" as savage anachronisms. But as I turn to the bloody task at hand, I suffer no sickening sympathy for my prey. My uniquely human empathy—intense feelings of love, of shared circumstance and common fate—is visceral. Gazing at this gorgeous beast, my eyes cloud with water and I accept this without shame. Yet and at the same time, I am positively electrified, buzzing with what Ortega y Gasset calls the "good hunter's almost mystical agitation." This, too, I accept without shame.

I draw my knife and begin the gritty task of making meat: unzip hide, open belly, plunge in both arms to the elbows and struggle by Braille to set free a hundred pounds of steaming organs, which I ritually inspect and attempt to name, as if performing an internal inventory on myself. As always, I'm awestruck by the rock-hard muscularity of the heavy heart.

Hart's blood. Heart's blood. Heartsblood . . . warm and wet on trembling hands.

I bag the meat in four pillowcase-sized sailcloth bags and hang it high from sturdy ponderosa limbs, hoarding it from my fellow forest carnivores. Tomorrow, my friend Erica and I will make two, maybe three slow trips up and down this mountain to pack out every last scrap of deboned meat and the small but artful antlers.

A job of work it is, and I love it. Like getting in my winter's wood, all ten cords of it, or gathering mushrooms, nuts, wild onions, and berries, this traditional brand of hard work is good hard work, what Pulitzer poet and former bowhunter Gary Snyder calls "real work," in that it exercises the spirit as well as the body. Unlike a city friend's precocious young son who recently felt compelled to ask "Daddy, who killed this chicken we're eating?" I know where the meat on my table comes from, and at precisely what costs to all concerned. Taken in this grateful spirit, each meal of self-got wild meat is at once precious memory and sacrament.

In the end, we find sacredness only where we seek it, and only if we seek it. True hunters, spiritual hunters—a minority, but a growing and maturing minority—seek and find sacredness in aspen grove and piney wood, in mountain meadow, rocky canyon, and rushing stream, and yes, in blood-stained hands.

The Short End of the Harpoon
——*'Asta Bowen*

I went to the Makah Nation because I wanted to see the end of the world. There's something irresistible about extremes, and Cape Flattery, at the far northwest corner of the Lower 48, was an extreme I had to go to. There between the Olympic Mountains and the Pacific Ocean lay the modest fishing village of Neah Bay, which I visited, the ancient settlement of Ozette, which I did not, and a winding coastal trail out to the cape. Report from the end of the world: It's windy out there.

Now, five years later, the prevailing wind from the Makah Nation is a roar of rhetoric. The tribe has decided to hunt whales again, after some seventy years, igniting a world-class controversy. The crux of the argument, according to *Mother Jones* magazine, comes down to "multiculturalists and environmentalists" who can't agree "whether it's more important to save whales or Indian culture."

This should be a non-dilemma. Both whales and Indian culture are important; both should be preserved. With the gray whale recovered to a population of 20,000, if the Makah can meet their needs with the harvest of five whales per year approved by the International Whaling Commission, what is the problem?

One problem is that some folks couldn't care less about either whales or Indians and would cheerfully sit back and watch the multiculturalists and environmentalists duke this one out—preferably to the death. It's one battle the reactionaries can't lose. Between the whalers, the whales, and the antiwhaling activists, someone else is bound to come out on the short end of the harpoon.

Another problem is that somewhere along the way to saving the whales, in the past few decades, the whales also saved us. In order to halt our extinction of these great species, we had to lose the image of the whale as mere commodity or enemy. As we got to know whales differently, roiling waters no longer meant a threat to old Jonah or even a light for our lamps. Thanks to conservation campaigns like Save the Whales, we came to see marine mammals as kin: members of the living family of our blue planet.

Once we forged a bond with the whale—as blubbery and barnacled a relative as one could hope to find in the family tree—links to other wildlife were easy to make. The bear was kin, and so was wolf; sea otter and seal, whooping crane, and (dare I say?) spotted owl were all valued members of the family, deserving of respect and worthy, when in danger, of saving. In this way the whale saved us, too—from arrogance, from loneliness, from the destruction of self through the destruction of habitat. Now, when we picture the whale, it is as a friend: rising sociably to meet the tour boat, turning a lazy eye to the filmmaker, or, in a warm Baja lagoon, giving birth as we do.

This is the whale we do not want to die. This is the whale we do not want the Makah to kill. And if the hunters are, as they promise, "pure of heart," this whale is not in danger. But we find that difficult to believe.

Friends, there's a culture in trouble here, and it's not the Makah. There's a culture that cannot believe a tribe could be motivated by something other than financial greed. There is a culture that has learned to kill without reverence and consume without celebration. There is a culture so removed from the earth, so completely symbolic, that it accepts the image of a whale and the reality of a whale as interchangeable: equally powerful, equally meaningful.

In this society there are commentators who can, with a straight face, reduce "culture, values, [and] traditions" to P.R. buzzwords. There are writers who assume that 55 percent unemployment can't be all that bad in a town with two motels, Federal Express, and the all-important espresso bar. There are people who think poverty must be abject and malnutrition fatal before subsistence becomes a "legitimate" issue.

We are, inevitably, products of our experience. As a young woman one generation removed from Iceland, I visited that windy end of the world and watched, one morning, as a whale disappeared from the dock of my cousin's village. The blubber was stripped and the meat sold in scores of neat plastic bags. The baleen, I remember, made coveted playthings for the kids. With the family cod boat full of fish, we didn't eat whale that night. If we had, I wouldn't have liked it. I wasn't hungry enough. I couldn't remember.

The Makah are hungry enough to remember. I wish them a pure heart, safe passage, and the grace to save the whale they must kill.

Bison in the Snow
—Andrea Barnett

Seventy-five-miles-per-hour winds pushed the first snowstorm of the season through Paradise Valley recently, rattling the windows of my home forty miles north of Yellowstone National Park. I like snow, but these clouds are a deadly portent: They mean bison are migrating, leaving the park's boundaries in search of food. Standing to meet them at the border are Montana's Department of Livestock officials.

As of Christmas Eve, the agency was "hazing" bison, pushing them off national forest land back into the park. It's an exercise that's been repeated 600 times so far this season, according to Director Marc Bridges, though he notes many of these are the same animals, hazed over and over again.

Bison advocates complain such treatment stresses the animals, making it difficult for them to survive the bitter Northern Rockies winters. Yet as the weather worsens, those same livestock employees will turn to deadlier methods. Any day now, when the snow piles up deep enough, they will cease hazing and pick up guns, ready to repeat a sordid chapter in Montana's history.

I remember it well. It was early morning in April 1997 when I ventured back into Yellowstone's Hayden Valley after a long, harsh winter, short days made all the darker by death. Upward of 2,000 bison died that season, and a close friend succumbed to cancer. This day was sunny, and my two companions and I were on cross-country skis; we had to scurry to get into the backcountry before the snow got too soft to navigate.

Our destination was a thermal area at the south end of the valley, one not accessible by boardwalks. As we arrived, the familiar smell of sulfur hung on the air. Pausing, we caught another scent: the fetor of ethyl mercaptan from rotting meat. The carcass itself, a bison, was almost hidden from view, lying in a dip between two hills. We decided to pay our respects.

This was one of hundreds of bison who starved that year, when heavy snows buried forage too deep for the animals to excavate. The biggest villain that year was not the weather, though, but the State of Montana. In a few short months, government sharpshooters gunned down more than 1,100 of the great beasts.

Officials justified the slaughter on the grounds of preventing the spread of brucellosis, a disease brought to North America by cattle and carried by bison and elk. While there's never been any documented spread of brucellosis from bison back to cattle in the wild, the state nevertheless drew an invisible line at the park's boundary. Those that crossed the line in search of food were treated like livestock: tagged, radio-collared, penned up, and, much too often, killed. (Elk, beneficiaries of a strong hunting lobby, escaped a similar fate.)

When the killing began in earnest that January, the concert of death was joined by the close college friend of mine who was losing a five-year battle with lymphoma. As the body count at the park's boundaries rose, Brendan continued to decline. I got the call early one morning, just two days after visiting him at his parents' home in Cleveland, and knew he was gone; at that instant his death was linked inextricably in my mind to the madness unfolding in news reports every day from the park.

I kept watch from my home and made the trip south regularly to ski the more accessible Lamar Valley. Most of the bison I saw were gathered near the park's northern entrance, their ribs showing. By spring, more than half of the herd was gone.

It was not until that April trip into the backcountry that winter's nightmarish qualities began to dissipate. I took solace in seeing the evidence of bears feeding off that first carcass. I took off my gloves and touched its fur. It was a quiet resting spot, and at that moment I began to see the peace in its death and in Brendan's.

Natural death is one thing, state-sponsored slaughter quite another. As the holidays approach this year, forecasters are once again predicting bad weather, and the State of Montana is completing a plan to continue the slaughter for another fifteen years.

Yesterday, friends and I made a quick trip into Lamar Valley. There, we watched a wolf pack lounging half a mile from a small herd of bison near Slough Creek. An incredible treat, though I couldn't help but think of the bison capture facility that livestock officials are building near West Yellowstone, on the opposite side of the park. There, they will shoot all pregnant females. They will test all others for brucellosis and shoot those with the disease.

The radio reports that another storm is due in tonight. The killing season has begun.

Fencing the Wild
—*Hal Walters*

It looked like a rock anchoring the barbed-wire fence, the same way rocks anchor fences all over the West. Then I saw it move. As I drew closer, I saw that the "rock" was a spotted elk calf hanging from the fence by its front leg.

The scene was grisly. Apparently the herd had crossed the shiny new fence, but this calf had gotten caught in the wire and had been left behind. The bottom two strands were coated in blood and hair for two feet in either direction. The calf's front leg was held firmly, the wires twisted around it. The sun was dehydrating the animal, and the flies had closed in to gnaw at the still-living flesh where the skin had been peeled away by the wire and its razor-sharp barbs.

Many people get hurt trying to release wildlife from fences, so I approached slowly and carefully. The safest way to release an animal is to stand back and cut the wires, but the only tool I had was a Buck knife. Using my bare hands, I pried the wires apart wide enough to free the leg. The hoof slid through and dropped to the ground.

The elk calf let out a faint, pathetic squeal.

The West used to be a land of sprawling ranches divided by miles and miles of barbed-wire fences. Most stockmen had too much fence line and too little money to make a big deal out of fences. They used juniper fence posts and three strands of wire, the statutory definition of a "fence" in some states.

Now many of these ranches have been subdivided into thirty-five- and forty-acre ranchettes, and the owners of these parcels fence in a few cows or horses. This accounts for many, many more miles of fence—it takes one mile to surround a forty-acre ranchette. In Colorado's Custer County, where I live, there are roughly 1,000 such ranchettes. This could translate into a thousand miles of new fence if all the owners were to stretch some wire.

Worse yet, many westerners—both newcomers and old-timers—don't know how to build a fence that will keep livestock inside while allowing wildlife to pass safely. The fence that caught this elk calf had been recently built across an historic elk thoroughfare. The owners are not full-time residents and probably haven't spent enough time on their land to know how many elk regularly cross it.

Through its Habitat Partnership Program, the Colorado Division of Wildlife helps landowners make the right decisions when it comes to dealing with wildlife-habitat issues. The program sponsors Habitat Partnership Committees that deal with these issues on a local basis and distributes a booklet, *Fences for Man and Beast.*

In deer, elk, and antelope country, this booklet recommends fence heights of forty to forty-two inches. The top two strands should be spaced twelve inches apart so that adult deer and elk will have less of a chance of becoming entangled when jumping. Smooth wire is recommended for the top strand.

The bottom strand should also be smooth wire, placed at least sixteen to eighteen inches above the ground so that deer fawns, elk calves, and antelope of all ages can pass beneath freely. (Even adult pronghorns do not jump fences but crawl under them instead.) If more people used these fencing guidelines, fewer critters would wind up twisted in wire like the elk calf that I found.

Some passing motorists stopped and held a blanket over the calf for shade. After a while, the little elk started to rock side to side, mustering the energy to stand. Suddenly it bounced to its feet, turned wildly, and slammed back into the fence. It bounced off the tight wires, spun around in the opposite direction, and started up a steep ridge.

We watched the elk calf climb. Every now and then it paused, and I expected it to collapse. Instead it seemed to gather more strength with every stop, until it at last trotted over the ridge's summit.

I'm not so naïve as to think this was a Hollywood ending. The calf was very young and the predators are very many. Also, the cuts were an opening for infection. But elk are extremely hardy animals, and if by some fate of nature the calf was rejoined with its herd that evening, it might have a chance.

In a region where uniform building codes are often a hot topic of debate, a uniform fencing code seems more necessary. It only took one look into the eyes of an elk calf to convince me.

Hope in the Garden
—*Marty Jones*

I can hear the rain falling, the swollen drops slapping the pavement like fish stranded on a beach. For gardeners anywhere else, this would be cause for celebration, but not for those of us at elevation. Here on the High Plains, rain on the window can quickly become hail on the hollyhocks, turning glorious horticulture to swamps of green confetti and mothballs.

This is but one of the hurdles facing the gambler who dares to garden in the Rocky Mountain West, where the growing season can be summed up with one harsh reality: "These are the times that try men's soils."

Since I moved to Colorado a few years ago, I've killed more living things than global combat and buried more dead than a funeral director. My thumbs, emerald green back East, have turned black, their touch as poisonous as Roundup. Based on the number of plants I've purchased, the staff at my local nursery thinks I'm living on a farm and not some tiny plot in sight of Denver's skyline. Little do my smiling enablers know of my need to purchase in pairs, like some flora-collecting Noah, since my first plantings of nearly everything meet an early death.

The problem is that very things that nurture life at lower altitudes conspire to commit mass murder at higher ones. Sun, heat, and precipitation all combine to turn crops to compost and dreams of backyard veggies to trips to the local farmer's market. Closer to sea level, the rays of the sun gently coax plants up from the ground and on to fruition. At four-digit altitudes, an angry orb unobstructed by atmosphere turns green to brown and fresh herbs to dried. Each day is a plant-world talent show, where enthusiastic newcomers wilt like open-stage rookies, cooked under the first rays of limelight.

Looking for a million-dollar idea? How about sunscreen for the photosynthesis set? I could fill a composter the size of downtown with the greenery I've broiled, in spite of weeks of hardening off. Even my most toughened plants, deliberately moved in and out of the house for weeks, fade fast under the western sky. As soon as the sun shines, their leaves crack and burn like the foreheads of out-of-towners in Coors Field's sunny seats.

Don't buy the theory that these premature passings make for heartier plants next year. Instead, the new crop displays genetically transmitted fear and loathing. My seedlings from last year's toasted tithonia plants are still squatting an inch above ground, refusing to grow up fast only to die young at the top of the fence.

Wide-ranging temperatures wreak havoc as well. For starters, you've got to spare your plants from spring's frosty chill and snowdrifts piled inside your "wall of water" force fields. If your tomato plants are lucky enough to survive that test, the heat will do its own damage weeks later, stewing your precious Early Girls right on the vine.

Hail may be the worst culprit of them all. After finally gaining a foothold, last season's flowers were stripped bare by shrapnel-sized missives from on high. I'll never forget the horrible sight of my beloved morning glories floating in a swirling, multicolored soup of hail. I can still hear the flowers screaming as I struggled to cover them with plastic sheeting, their cries blending with the roar of marbles pounding the bucket over my head. My exposed neck still bears scars.

Ah, but despite the daunting obstacles and the painful memories from the previous year, like an aging quarterback, we somehow manage to come back for one more shot. In my heart I can still feel the pain of turning under another season cut short, but with a picture of a smiling number seven in my mind, I'm confident this year could be my championship season.

Outside, another crop of sugar snaps is squinting into the sky and straining upward, while my okra puts on weight for the fight to come. The broader leaves of my Swiss chard are again valiantly giving up the ghost, sacrificing themselves for their younger, tender kin. No matter what the birds may whisper to them, my new team of sunflowers is gallantly stretching for a better angle on the blue brilliance above.

Once again there's a shovel by the back door, dirt under my fingernails, and hope in the garden.

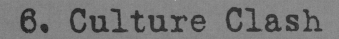

6. Culture Clash

We Got Your Number, Cowboy

—Jim Dwyer

He was big. Tall big with a beer belly, flushed face, and hair faded into the color of dog markings in the snow.

"Carpetbaggers!" he spat at me and my staff as we prepared to hand out 911 address plaques to residents of the Whetstone area of Cochise County in southeastern Arizona. This was our sixth year into the project of addressing Cochise County, some 6,300 square miles. The addressing was needed for an enhanced 911 system and for the U.S. Postal Service, all the commercial delivery services, and all utilities.

The big fellow in front of me couldn't, wouldn't, try to understand why we were doing this, this invasion of his right not to have an address.

"Carpetbaggers!" he spat again. "My people have been here for a hundred years. What right do you carpetbaggers have to tell us what to do?"

We'd seen a bunch of his type over the years while driving the back roads of Cochise County. People who just don't give a damn if 911 ever finds them. Don't give a damn for nothing except those who share their double-wide and their assortment of animals.

"Hey, mister," I looked at him. "Why don't you go tell all that to the Apaches? They said the same thing to your ancestors, only they called them white eyes instead of carpetbaggers."

He spat and mumbled a bit more and then stomped from the firehouse that we were using for the day, cursing everyone and everything he came across. Some of the folks who were waiting politely in line giggled, saying, "Oh, that's him alright. He's always grumpin' about somethin'."

It's a shame to see the hunting grounds of the Chiricahua Apaches, of Cochise and Geronimo, being numbered by the White Man. It would be a bigger shame, we try to explain to ranchers, farmers, active and retired military, New Age hippies, and the gaggle of counterculture types who have been gripped by the magnetism of Cochise County, if someone got run over by a pickup, shot by a jealous mate, or awakened by a heart attack and the 911 units couldn't find them because the roads weren't named or marked, no addresses were visible, or the dusty wash they were trying to run an ambulance through wasn't on the maps.

If addressing hasn't hit your part of the Wild West, it will. All us real or wannabe cowboys and cowgirls and big-city transplants will be hanging green-and-white address plaques on our fences, houses, and businesses so that underpaid emergency medical technicians, sheriff's deputies, and volunteer firefolk can rush to our rescue, whether we want them to or not. If they can't find us, someone will sue the chaps off the county, beyond the level of insurance coverage. We could be fixing roads with rocks and brooms as our taxes soar and our sun-washed paradise turns into a financial purgatory.

The benefits? All this addressing will improve the chances of your mobile home being delivered to the right parcel, will allow delivery services to get your medication to you while you are still breathing, and will potentially lower your home insurance rates as fire protection becomes more certain.

It's not all money, litigation, and invasion of privacy. There is a light side. Like the time my staffer Sally and I drove up to an isolated mobile home surrounded by mesquite and high-desert grasses. Sally, who was probably a lion tamer in a past life, peered out the window of our county GMC Jimmy, her flowered straw hat whipping in the autumn wind, and exhaled, "Oh my god!"

On the weathered porch of the old mobile, a skinny cowboy rose like a shot from a big bucket, holding a towel to cover his essentials, his battered ten-gallon hat dipped in deference.

"'Scuse me," offered Sally as I smiled from behind the wheel, "Do you have an address for your place?"

"Ma-ma'am?"the aging cowboy sputtered, still standing at attention. "I didn't know I was supposed to have an address. I was just cleanin' up to go to town. I haven't been there in three weeks and got kinda low on supplies."

Ignoring the cowboy's predicament, Sally kept him at attention until she got his name and asked for his telephone number. He just shook his head. "Ain't got no phone. Never saw the need for one. If I do, I go to the neighbors over yonder," he pointed to a nice little spread about a mile south. Sally gave him her two-minute drill on why he should have a telephone, then looked hard at him and said, "You better get dressed, before you catch cold."

"Yes, ma'am. Thank you, ma'am," he said, slowly sinking into his big bucket as I headed the Jimmy back to the road. Sally finally laughed out loud and I wondered what was going through the mind of that poor old cowboy, wondered if Cochise and Geronimo were looking down from the rolling Chiricahua Mountain Range and laughing, too, at the foolish white eyes numbering paradise.

A Wardrobe for the New West
—*Louise Wagenknecht*

I can count on the fingers of one hand the new clothes I've bought in the past five years: a set of insulated coveralls, underwear, felt liners for my snow boots, gloves. All the rest came from yard sales and the kind of thrift shops where you walk past the eight-track tapes and mismatched plastic plates on your way to the clothes.

I visited my favorite shop this fall during their semiannual bag sale. The crowd was small and genteel: two California emigrés looking for campy Halloween costumes. Discovering a taffeta formal in a blinding shade of pink, they fell shrieking into each other's arms while I dug resolutely through racks of polyester pantsuits. I uncovered a plaid Pendleton wool jacket in the classic double-breasted style, just like the one my grandmother bought in 1953. It had all the original buttons and no apparent moth holes. The prom queens stopped squealing and looked at me.

"That," one of them purred, "would be worth a lot of money at this vintage clothing place I know over in Sun Valley."

I smiled but said nothing. I can't even afford used clothes in Sun Valley.

"If you want to sell that, I work over at XYZ Realty," she caroled as she left. She and her companion were, I noticed, still wearing their California office clothes. Perhaps a few years of living three hours from even the nearest Sears would teach them humility and send those tasteful gray suits into the closet for funerals. Perhaps.

It's hard to hate people whose castoffs keep me clad above my station in life. Thanks to their donations to this shop, run by the local humane society, I sport brands I couldn't otherwise afford. I run into my friends here, too, and we are not ashamed.

I wear the surplus wealth of Sunbelt refugees, the gleanings of a thousand malls. At the annual wine-tasting benefit, I sip merlot and feel *très chic* in a secondhand Shetland sweater. As a string quartet wails, I feel eyes boring into my back and turn as someone thin and tan tries to decide where she's seen the sweater before. When she remembers, she will despise me, a barbarian at the gates.

Go back to Palm Springs if you don't like it, I sneer silently, gobbling more brie and wishing I'd worn my yard-sale Bay-to-Breakers T-shirt. Not that I ever actually ran a marathon, you understand. It just happens to look good on me since I got the flu during lambing season and lost all that weight.

Something weird has happened here. While sales of retail clothing are flat, thrift shops sell almost-new sweaters for pennies. Raised by a mother and grandmother who avoided used clothing even in the Depression, brought up in the prosperous mid-century decades, I virtually stopped buying new clothes in the late 1970s. Wages and farm prices stagnated in the West; the cost of everything else didn't.

Now every week brings newcomers to this land of low wages, depressed cattle prices, a dying timber industry, and a nervous mining climate. A dollar goes further here, if you have the dollar to begin with. Fleeing the dense air and dark peoples of California or Denver or Phoenix, the immigrants arrive flush with real-estate cash and celebrate by cleaning out their closets. We watch and wait, votresses of a new cargo cult.

Sometimes when I leave the thrift shop, I see a van bearing the mantra "We Buy Levis" parked a couple of blocks away on Main Street. Remembering a denim jacket at home, I wonder how much it's worth and consider returning to this fin-de-siècle shrine of the New West to find out.

It's just a work jacket to me, not a fashion statement or an American icon. It's a little frayed, and stained, and I ripped the pocket out on a fence post one day, but when I bought it, it was new, and the world held more of everything. If I sell it now, I'll never get it back. I guess I don't need a tank of gas that badly. Not yet.

Cowboy Poetry Stinks
—*Mark Matthews*

"Most cowboy poetry stinks."

Just hold on, before you bash me over the head with your ten-gallon hat, pardner. Those aren't my words. They came from Montana's cowboy poet laureate, Wallace McRae, who I interviewed a few years ago, just before the state bestowed on him its most prestigious literary prize, the H. G. Merriam Award.

McRae went on to describe cowboy poetry as the garage sale of literature. "Once in a while you find a real bargain," he said.

Last week, more than 10,000 cowboy poetry fans rounded up to listen for those treasures at the fourteenth annual Cowboy Poetry Gathering in Elko, Nevada. I've never been to Elko, but a few years ago I did attend the Montana gathering in Lewistown.

Men and women from ten to eighty years old, rawhide-skinned and lily-white, soft-spoken and gruff, all took turns reciting at the podium during the morning and afternoon workshops. For many, it seemed a tough transition—from tight-lipped, independent cowboy to sensitive, vulnerable poet. Most were more comfortable lamenting over a long-departed horse than revealing their personal failings or longings. There was a considerable lack of passion and emotion, unless it was for some colorful sunset or prairie grassland.

Others dropped all pretension of insight or intellectualism and just tried to tell amusing stories in rhymed couplets. McRae was correct in his assessment. Most of it was boring, especially when recited in a preschool, sing-song cadence.

Who was I to judge? I used to write bad poetry, too. Only I never let anyone read it, and I stopped creating it. At least these folks put themselves out there, and they seemed to write for the love of creation, not to try to make a literary impression as I had. They simply said, to the best of their abilities, "These are my experiences as a human being living in this god-forsaken, blessed-by-heaven world of the West. No more, no less."

I applauded their efforts.

There were moments when some wizened rancher, whose library probably consisted of the collected works of Louis L'Amour, cleverly turned an imaginative phrase or painted a colorful metaphor that was as enchanting and inspiring as anything Shakespeare ever wrote. Then the polite applause turned into enthusiastic recognition for a true artist in the rough.

Despite some great artistic successes by such poet pioneers as Badger Clark, John Grafton Rodgers, and D. J. O'Malley and contemporaries such as McCrae, Paul Zarzyski, and Henry Realbird, academics continue to shun cowboy poetry. When McCrae received his award, many of the Montana literati were stupefied. The following was a typical response by a University of Montana English professor.

"Cowboy poetry confirms your expectations rather than stretching the way you think about things. It's very comforting to think in clichés, but let's not pretend that it's art."

Cowboy poets don't care what the stuffed shirts say. "Everything's right out there," McRae explained. "They [academics] don't like that because there's nothing left for them to interpret."

Cowboy poetry could be the most popular form of folk art being practiced today. When was the last time more than 10,000 people jammed a university campus or small town for a weekend to listen to visiting poets, as they do at Elko? McRae says many people prefer cowboy poetry because they are sick of the "nonrepresentational or impressionistic mysteries devoid of meaning, meter, or rhyme that are being written and called poetry."

The numbers not only prove him right, but some cowboy poetry gems hold their own with the greatest creations in literature. Just read some of Badger Clark's works, like "Spanish Is a Loving Tongue" and "The Outlaw." Clark was born in the Dakota Territory in 1883. In the first two verses of "The Outlaw," a cowboy brags about being able to rope any wild steer or break any defiant horse, but in the end he admits to having trouble coping with a different breed of animal.

When the devil at rest underneath my vest
Gets up and begins to paw
And my hot tongue strains at its bridle reins,
Then I tackle the real outlaw.
When I get plumb riled and my sense goes wild

And my temper is fractious growed,
If he'll hump his neck just a triflin's speck,
Then it's dollars to dimes I'm throwed.

Though the gems are rare, it's still worthwhile attending a cowboy poetry gathering, especially the workshops for amateurs. You'll see real people attempting to create art. That's rare enough these days.

Throwing the Dice
on Our Kids' Future

—*Mary Sojourner*

"This Is Our Kids' Inheritance." I saw the bumper sticker the first time on the back of a beat-up old Airstream in a Searchlight, Nevada, casino parking lot, and I thought of one of my dad's favorite sayings: "Enjoy your money and your kids while you're alive."

He didn't and died with that regret. I'm fifty-nine. Writing is not work from which you retire voluntarily, and if I died this second, my kids would inherit nine full bookcases, a paid-for 1990 four-cylinder Nissan pale-blue pickup with raven wings painted on the doors, hundreds of audio tapes, and as many geodes, fire agates and slabs, chunks and chips of obsidian as fit in a two-room cabin.

I have thirty-six cents in my pocket, an obligatory $50 in my credit union savings account, $43.72 left in overdraft privilege, and more bills than I can think about. There is one reason, one reason alone, for my financial condition. Not shopping. Not travel. Not good works. I am a slot hog.

Nickel machines. Super Sevens. Black Rhino. Kitty Keno. I read a checklist today that tells you if you're a compulsive gambler. Four yesses means you better lock yourself and your liquid assets in the closet. I hit six out of ten, which in Keno would win a lousy four nickels and in real life means trouble.

I'm thinking hard about all of this, not because I believe I can quit but because I spent three nights and two days of the holidays in a Nevada "gaming" town. I was surrounded by old people, from the slot-machine seat upon which my butt seemed to be welded, to the benches outside the back of the casinos, where there's a colony of savvy feral cats that have gotten so fussy they turn up their noses at anything other than shrimp or steak.

Most of the old people were women. Most wore pastel jogging suits appliquéd with sparkly kittens, Christmas trees, dice, aces and jacks, and logos from Palm Springs, Scottsdale, San Diego, and Atlantic City. They loved to talk, especially if their hubbies were somewhere else, especially if they were dead.

They rarely drank the free, watery booze the cocktail waitresses, most of whom are my age, brought around, and they almost never played off the credits on the machines. Ching ching ching, one by one, they dropped the nickels in the slots. When they hit, they cashed out. When they lost, they pulled another twenty dollars out of their purses and hollered, "Change!"

They told me everything. "We just sold the place in Palm Springs. We've got a double-wide in Tucson and a double-wide in Columbus. When we're here, we stay in a little park motel down near Topoc. We had to sell the house in Palm Springs. It costs a fortune to keep up one of those places, plus, you know you can't get decent yard work done for decent wages the way you used to."

Their husbands play blackjack. One woman figures it costs her and her husband about $30,000 every winter for him to play blackjack. He won't admit it, but she keeps count.

I looked around. Old women, old men, black, Native American, Hispanic, white, white, white, and me. Our faces gray in the hectic light of our machines, our fingers placing into the pockets of a very few very rich people what we believe we've earned, be it a fortune, be it next month's rent. This is our kids' inheritance.

I looked at the old woman's sweet face. She set her hand on my arm. "My kids are all over the country," she said, "I miss them."

"How much do you see them?"

She shook her head. "They've got such busy lives. Careers. My grandkids. We get together maybe once a year."

"Are you close to the grandkids?"

"Oh no," she laughed. "Kids are so different these days. I used to try, but once they got to be near their teens, I just gave up."

It was my turn at the counter. I cashed my points in for twelve bucks, considered leaving, and didn't. While I lost my twelve bucks I thought about the word "inheritance." And the word "elder." By the time the last cluster of losing flowers and nines and rhinos dropped into place, I knew the inheritance we squander in casinos is not just money.

Those of us hunkered in front of our machines, bent over the craps table, are giving away our time, our knowledge, and our stories. What we might once have passed on to our children, our children's children, remains locked in our hearts and minds. We gather in casinos, in gated communities, in exclusive golf clubs, and leave the younger generations to piece together what they can. We never face the possibility that who we have become is ludicrous to them, disgusting, unnecessary.

I don't know how many younger people want to learn to write an elegant sentence, make Pennsylvania Dutch chicken soup, live on next to nothing, face down fear, see through a con, tell their heart's truth. I'm blessed to have children who do.

I don't know whether I can continue, as I have for a week, to wade through the disaster of my checkbook, admit this addiction to a few friends, and keep myself out of the little casino forty miles south. I am blessed to be haunted by an unlikely ghost, a bumper sticker that reads, "This Is Our Kids' Inheritance." For now, it seems the lesser terror.

High Time for a New West Celebration
—*Ed Quillen*

This year, every town big enough to boast a high school, and more than a few that have trouble keeping a post office in business, hosted a festival.

Even though these small-town celebrations go by different names—Wild West Days, Gold Rush Days, Pioneer Weekend, Founders' Day, Old West Festival—they hold much in common: They all focus on the Old West.

The parades offer a caravan of horse-drawn wagons. The men sport vests, derbies, and sleeve garters. The women wear demure hoopskirts or provocative dance-hall corselets. Children wander about in suspended knickers or frilly bonnets. A few ersatz bandits, toting thumb-buster revolvers loaded with blanks, pretend to rob the bank or a stagecoach.

The festival generally includes a contest of Old West skills—riding and roping at a rodeo, for instance, or single- and double-jack drilling to honor the hard-rocking mining days. A few towns even have "cussin', belchin', and spittin'" contests.

Not that there's anything wrong with such festivals, but they're seldom distinctive. These days, with rural western towns all competing for tourist dollars, the town with the courage to try something different should come out ahead. So why not, instead of an Old West weekend, a New West weekend in some gentrifying hamlet where art galleries and coffee bars have replaced hardware stores and feed shops?

Old West weekends often focus on a prominent event in a town's history—the first settlers, a big silver strike, the arrival of the railroad, or a battle that led to the expulsion of the people who had been there before the pioneers claimed the spot.

A New West weekend might similarly commemorate an event that started the transition: the 1968 arrival of the first VW microbus with offbeat paint and a driver with a headband, the 1971 opening of the eatery that served organic sprouts and went broke within the year, the 1974 founding of an alternative newspaper or community radio station.

Other important historic events could be reenacted through the New West weekend: the 1969 battle between the indigenous good ol' boys, who were armed with axe handles and hay hooks, against the hippie commune on the hill. Or the first known bust of a marijuana cultivator in 1974. Or the municipal election of 1978, when the new folks took over the town government with the promise to install mellow cops, who still haven't materialized.

There is a problem with this approach—we don't yet have the historical perspective. We don't know whether the arrival of hippies thirty years ago was the precursor of the arrival of the New West in the 1990s. The two invasions might not be related at all.

Indeed, it could be that the events properly worth celebrating at a New West weekend would be more recent: "First 10,000-square-foot house occupied less than one month a year," "First restaurant with minuscule servings and a long wine list to go totally smoke-free," or "Last time a two-bedroom shotgun house on a postage-stamp lot rented for less than $1,000 a month."

No matter what seminal New West event the organizers select, they should still hold contests—for New West skills, rather than Old West trades, of course.

Why watch some ranch hand on a bronco when horses are as obsolete as typewriters? Especially when you could watch sport-ute drivers maneuver through an obstacle course while maintaining constant cell-phone conversation and consulting their GPS navigation aids?

Why celebrate the archaic skills of working-class miners as they drill and muck before a crowd that doesn't know a stope from a winze? The New West working class could show off its modern skills: bed-making, toilet-scrubbing, burger-flipping, lift-attending, drink-mixing—with a grand finale race for the hills when INS agents make a surprise appearance to round up undocumented immigrants.

Throw in a UFO sighting, an espresso tasting, some sweat-lodge demonstrations, and a few minutes of arcane chanting as every celebrant holds hands in a mystic circle. Cap it all with a parade—no floats, bands, or horses but instead a cavalcade of conspicuous consumption, featuring $80,000 land yachts towing $40,000 sport utes towing $20,000 boats.

Come to think of it, though, that's pretty much how things are now on most weekends. That might explain why no town has announced a New West festival yet—why bother with the work of organizing and marketing a festival, when one seems to be happening all on its own?

Junk: The West's Best Friend
—*Don Olsen*

Our little county in rural Colorado, like many in the mountain West, recently adopted a new junk ordinance that outlaws the accumulation of old tires, cars, and trailers by people (mostly newcomers) who believe it's a God-given property right to be able to transform their tiny ranchettes into Mad-Max–like postapocalyptic junk zones.

This often infuriates the neighbors, who don't appreciate having their view of the mountains blocked by trash and their property values destroyed when Ma and Pa Kettle move in next door.

I can understand why the county wants to protect its more responsible property owners from this invasion of the unkempt, but I also believe the commissioners are doing exactly the wrong thing.

Our agriculture-oriented valley is one of the last in western Colorado to have escaped the attention of the real-estate developers who are busy transforming the rest of the state's ranch lands into tract subdivisions and tacky retail strips for the nation's wealthy—who want to build second homes here.

It's only a matter of time before the developers find us, and the only hope we may have of not becoming the next Aspen or Jackson Hole is to pretend we're hopeless hillbillies viciously opposed to all efforts at tastefulness, civilization, and planned-unit development.

I think the commissioners should pass a junk ordinance that actually encourages clutter, rubbish, and other socially degenerate behavior. The commissioners could even establish a point system that rewards bad taste. For example:

—Junk vehicles in your front yard: 5 points per vehicle.

—Dismantled vehicle engines in your front yard: 8 points.

—Modular houses: 5 points; double-wides: 10 points; beat-up trailers: 12 points; beat-up trailers used as chicken houses: 20 points.

—Loud gravel pits located next to state scenic byways: 20 points; auto-repair shops along scenic byways: 15 points; roadside signs that say, "If you can read this, you're in my crosshairs!": 50 points.

—Wooden butterflies prominently displayed on side of house or shed: 5 points per insect.

—Chain-link fencing: 10 points.

—Chain-link fencing with dog behind it: 20 points (30 points if the dog is rabid).

—Signs that read, "Kitty cat hunting allowed": 10 points.

—Using the John Deere for grocery trips: 15 points.

—Topped trees: 25 points.

—Electric utility substations prominently displayed along scenic roadways: 30 points (if substations are illuminated at night by high-powered sodium vapor lights: 60 points).

—Animal carcasses hung in front yards: 15 points.

—Self-storage businesses along scenic byways: 30 points.

—Storage businesses using old trailers or decrepit shipping containers as lockers: 50 points.

—Tourism signs that say "Welcome to Our County—We're a Mess and Proud of It!": 30 points.

—Tourism signs that say "Welcome to Our County—Please Don't Stop for Detention Center Escapees": 50 points.

—Tourism signs that say "Welcome to Our County, Home of the Famous Elk Penis Walking Stick!": 40 points.

I think if we play our cards right, most urban refugees will realize we're hopelessly tacky here and avoid us like the plague. Maybe they'll just head on over the hill to Telluride.

In Praise of Trailer Trash
—Dewey Linze

In the mid-1930s, when poverty had a stranglehold on the country and sliced bread was a nickel a loaf, we lived in a trailer park, or trailer court, and everyone outside of the encampment called us "trailer trash."

It was insulting and vilipending, but this was the way the "haves" set themselves apart from the "have-nots," or the trailer people. To the cops and welfare and truant officers, the trailer court was where all evil spawned and spread.

The old trailer, I remember, had no street address, and it was bare of heat, water, or electricity. It sat about fifty feet from the Missouri Pacific's main-line tracks in St. Louis, Missouri. The train noise was deafening, clacking wheels crossing the rail seams, day and night.

The hobos who knocked on the trailer doors to beg for a bite to eat were never turned away. More than a few were educated and proud men, young and old, and down on their luck.

Well, after many years, the scars of that era have healed over, although many of the trailer-trash kin died without ever knowing a cure was coming. At the end of World War II, my family sold the old trailer and came to California. I bought them a mobile home, a clean, three-bedroom, aluminum-sided house in a San Pedro, California, mobile-home park. It was our home until the beginning of the Korean War.

Trailer houses have vanished. Yet this rickety and fragile structure for poor families was the precursor to the mobile home, and the mobile home to what is now the manufactured home, built in a factory to a strict federal building code. Most neighborhood folks have seen changes in the construction technology, design, interiors and exteriors, siding materials, and roofs that compare with sited dwellings.

Manufactured housing is now a multibillion-dollar business, booming particularly loud in the West. In Arizona, the number of manufactured homes is 300,000. Nevada hosts 90,000, and California's tabulation is 600,000.

The growing strength of the industry reveals its most attractive characteristic—affordability.

In 1998, families in California, Colorado, Washington, Oregon, Montana, Arizona, Nevada, Idaho, New Mexico, and Wyoming spent more than $2.2 billion on 47,147 manufactured homes, the homes averaging $48,000 each. Now nearly one of every three new single-family homes built in the United States is a manufactured home. Twenty million Americans opted for the manufactured home to satisfy the unbridled craving for home ownership.

No politician in her or his right mind would dare to debunk manufactured homes after learning that 7 percent of the nation's population call them "home." Yet some still do, acting as the cowbells of tract-home builders and challenging every move to give manufactured homes the same recognition as sited homes.

Heads-up California was one of the first states to introduce and pass a law that permits manufactured homes to coexist with regular sited homes in a single neighborhood. In western communities, the fight continues between the haves and the have-nots, with some upscale towns still unwilling to allow mobile homes or even manufactured homes within city limits.

In other places, manufactured-home parks, where homeowners pay a nominal fee for spaces for their homes, are getting squeezed. In California, various agencies, authorizing fees for permits to build parks, have steadily increased them to the point that developers find them equal to the cost of carving the home space from raw land. As a result, the California parks are filling rapidly, and no new ones are on the drawing boards to remedy the situation to any appreciable degree.

That's unfortunate. Affordable housing is the foundation of the American dream, and manufactured housing offers Americans the best housing that a limited amount of money can buy.

The modern trailer park also offers something else increasingly rare in our society: a close sense of community. Manufactured-home park residents have a camaraderie that the dwellers of million-dollar home enclaves will never have. Over the years I have attended many Saturday afternoon potlucks at manufactured-home neighborhoods. At one, I counted over 200 entrées.

Such abundance was unheard of when I was a child, but the soulful honor of sharing and helping your neighbor remains the hallmark of "trailer trash" living.

Urban Soup for the Soul
—*Paul Krza*

I was on my way to a temporary move into the big city the other day when I got the bad news: You're going in the wrong direction.

That was the message when I stopped for gas on the outskirts of Denver. On the magazine stand, the cover of *Time* shouted, "Why more Americans are fleeing to SMALL TOWNS."

I had just left Wyoming, surely the essence of rural. With less than half a million people, it's the least populated U.S. state but still the size of some European countries. In fact, more people come to work in downtown Denver each day than live in both of Wyoming's two largest "cities."

A few days later, my *Washington Post National Weekly* arrived, touting the "Little Town on the Prairie," about "families returning to small towns." Was I making a big mistake, I wondered? Was I trading mecca for the urban jungle?

Over the past decade about 2 million people have moved from cities back to the small places, compared to about 1.4 million who went the other way in the previous decade. The shift is a familiar pattern for the West, where an influx in recent years has sparked explosive growth in many places. We've heard why this is happening. The small towns are "a great place to raise a family"; they are where "things slow down," where you can know the neighbors and don't have to lock your doors.

Moving back, slowing down. It has a nice romantic sound, but it ignores the realities of population growth everywhere. When people flock to rural places, they overwhelm them and destroy the small-place qualities they seek.

Living in urban places forces us to deal with each other, to find ways of sharing space and collectively tackling problems. More importantly, cities feed our human souls in ways that rural living just can't. They offer diversion and diversity, qualities I know are lacking in Wyoming.

A trip to a Denver supermarket offered me a first tantalizing glimpse. Different languages bounced off the produce. I shared aisle space with African-Americans and Latinos looking for cheese, paper towels, and light-bulbs. In Wyoming, which is virtually 90 percent-plus white, the people in the shops and streets look pretty much like each other. The phrase "nice place to raise a family" has a certain unfortunate racial-code ring to it.

The city opens minds and forces us to coexist. Next to the downtown streetcar stop, a street musician entertains. Gay newspapers are circulated openly. Crowded sidewalks test our space constraints. Going urban offers a stop at the Thai market for banana leaves, at the Russian-run European market for Slovak Kashkaval cheese, and at the store across from the mosque for curry spices. You can't find this stuff in rural, safe places.

"You're from Wyoming?" Yep, I admitted to a new acquaintance in Denver. "Not that many people there," she offered. "There's not much crime either," she added. "Well, surely not a whole lot of the street-type stuff or the shootings of police," I said, "but a recent survey showed methamphetamine use among youth in Wyoming was three times higher than national figures. Domestic violence is a big problem, and the state's suicide rate ranks high if not at the top of the rest of the states." "There's nothing to do here" goes the rural lament. Diversions may not cure, but they do smooth social ills.

The greatest thing about living in Wyoming, I tell folks, is that there aren't many people. The worst thing, I quickly add, is that there aren't many people. Sure, it's a real luxury to walk out into the Red Desert on a summer day and see nothing or to ski into the Wind River Mountains in the middle of winter and encounter white silence. Those are moments to be treasured as wonderful ways to rejuvenate the spirit, though, not to be lusted after by escapists who want to relive the same experience day after day.

Interestingly, many people who live in Wyoming often don't have a lot of time to enjoy the best stuff in the state—the fishing, the hunting, the great outdoors. The lousy economy has condemned lots of folks to two jobs. When they do get free moments, Wyomingites flee to Denver, Billings, and Salt Lake City.

The realities of civilization and human encounter—diversity and diversion—are in the cities, even with all their drawbacks. I think I was going in the right direction after all.

Always an Outsider
—Hal Clifford

It is sobering to experience an angry and resentful place. For fifteen years I was an insider, a local jeering newcomers to my overrun Colorado town. Then I moved to New Mexico and got the other end of the stick.

"Northern New Mexico is beautiful," mused my friend Burnie Arndt before we departed Aspen for Santa Fe. "I lived there. But I couldn't get work. I wasn't the right color. And if they don't like you, they'll burn you out of your house."

We laughed at him, of course. My wife and I were open-minded liberals, ready to embrace the multicultural experience. So we decamped from a ski-town condo to a sprawling adobe house at the end of a bumpy dirt road patrolled by mangy dogs and peopled by heavily armed neighbors.

There we began to learn the reality of the Land of Enchantment, which is this: Cultures in New Mexico don't blend so much as they abrade. Although the reasons for New Mexico's conflicts are unique to that state, the rest of the West is stratifying, too, fracturing along similarly brittle planes of income, privilege, and ethnicity.

Enormous friction exists in northern New Mexico between the very poor (generally Indian and Hispanic) and the very rich (generally Anglo). New Mexico is among the nation's poorest states, yet enclaves like Santa Fe attract mobile wealth. The result is a San Andreas Fault of social conflict that grinds the poor against the rich and produces anger, resentment, and stupendous rates of property crime, violence, and drunk driving—among the highest in the United States.

Northern New Mexico is beautiful yet impoverished, angry and dangerous. Illiteracy and alcoholism are pandemic. Rio Arriba County, north of Santa Fe, has a terrific heroin problem. Machismo and physical intimidation are quotidian facts of life. Crime is out of sight. I learned firsthand that it is hard to empathize in proper liberal fashion when you are afraid.

"I used to be a public defender," a young, Anglo assistant district attorney told me. "Then I got stabbed in the stomach. That kind of changed my attitude about crime."

I asked Craig Liebelt, the Anglo manager of a Santa Fe gallery, how he related to Hispanics after eight years of residency.

"I don't," he said. "They'll blame us for all their problems, but they're happy to take my monthly rent checks. I used to invite them to parties, all of that. And I never got anything back. So I stopped trying."

Charlie Carrillo, a Ph.D. and an award-winning carver of religious icons, is an Hispanic who says his culture does not value individual success. "*La envidia mata,*" he told me. "Envy kills." A 1994 book about his work as a santero brought him grief; other Hispanics began to resent him. "The more I seem to be in the public eye, the more I seem to be criticized," he said. "My wife, she cries probably once a week. That's the price we pay."

Reluctantly, we concluded after a year that New Mexico is not inclusive. New arrivals in the West typically find common ground in what drew them to a place: mineral wealth, homesteads, ski slopes. These common interests forge bonds among neighbors and foster a culture that says "Who you are is irrelevant if you care about what this place has to offer and give more than you take." Today, as always, much of the West offers immigrants a chance to make themselves anew on the basis of the life they build here. This is the essence of the American experience.

We saw a different version of the West in New Mexico—a culture that says that what matters is who you are, not why you are there. Unless your family is New Mexican you can never be a local, no matter how hard you try. People like us are always outsiders.

Places that are inclusive are vibrant—America has proved that to the world. Places that are exclusive tend to ossify. There's a lesson there for my old, increasingly angry and bitter hometown of Aspen, and for many western places that resent newcomers, whether they are from San Salvador, San Diego, or San Antonio. The gates around an unwelcoming community may be invisible, but they are nevertheless real and stultifying. The view from the outside, I learned, is not a pretty one.

"Loco" in Any Language
—*Stephen Lyons*

I almost ordered beef brains enchiladas.

Thank goodness for the bilingual menu at Tacos Michoacan. The waitress, who did not speak much English, was still able to point me toward the English-language section of the menu. A large-screen TV blared away, and I understood not a word of what appeared to be an emotional moment in a Spanish-language soap opera. Colorful, handmade belts from Mexico were displayed in a glass case below the cash register, next to cassettes of Mexico's hottest mariachi bands, and new calendars listing a Catholic saint for each day were printed in Spanish.

This all felt exotic and foreign, but I was in Caldwell, Idaho, one of the most diverse areas of a state well-known for discouraging diversity. Yet a visitor to southwestern Idaho at the end of the twentieth century will find agricultural-extension publications printed in both Spanish and English, along with signs in stores, schools, and courthouses. In the Nampa–Caldwell area, markets are stocked with Spanish-language books, magazines, videos, piñatas, and music cassettes. Translating is even a growth industry in Canyon County, paying up to forty dollars an hour.

Cinco de Mayo is the biggest event of the year in Caldwell, and the mayor, who is of Greek ancestry, would like it to become the largest celebration of any kind in Idaho.

"By being a very diverse community, it gives us opportunities that a lot of communities don't have," says Mayor Garret Nancolas. "If you have the opportunity to speak both languages you have an advantage. Most businesses are looking for bilingual employees to help mend and to bring together both communities."

If this is the future of Idaho, I'm all for it. Bilingualism, like diversity, is a way of life in southern Idaho despite efforts led by English-only fanatics such as Kootenai County's Ron Rankin, whose ruling last year declared his northern county English-only. Rankin sounds like the nineteenth-century British who, in their imperialistic fervor, hoped to purify the world for Christianity. God, after all, they reasoned, had to be a white Englishman.

Simon Winchester writes in *The Professor and the Madman*, "The equation was really very simple. . . . The more English there was in the world, the more God-fearing its peoples would be."

Bilingualism is here to stay for practical reasons. Idaho's Hispanic population has grown by 61 percent in seven years, from 52,927 in 1990 to 85,997 in 1997, according to the U.S. Census Bureau. The Idaho Commission on Hispanic Affairs lists eleven radio stations, two newspapers, and one television station. The emigration of peoples from one part of this great country to another is a strikingly American story, one that resonates with all of us who are the descendants of immigrants past and present.

However, Hispanics are hardly new. With such illustrious ancestors as the Aztecs, they certainly predate the European-language invasion. As historian Erasmo Gamboa once said, "We did not cross the border—the border crossed us."

To truly purify Idaho's foreign vocabulary one has to begin with Rankin's hometown of Coeur d'Alene. According to the book *Idaho Place Names* by Lalia Boone, the name comes from the French, who named the Native Americans of that area. "It has been interpreted in a variety of ways: 'awl,' 'pointed,' or 'needle-hearted.'" Let's rename the town "Dim Place of Below-Average Blowhards."

Coeur d'Alene Lake could be Lead Lake, to celebrate the tons of mine waste that line the lake bed. (Rank Lake might work, too, and be a fitting tribute to Rankin's legacy.)

A quick look through Boone's book reveals just how many names come from the French, the Spanish, and numerous Native American tribes: Shoshone, Orofino, Orogrande, Boise, Nampa, Latah, Palouse, Kuna, Acequia, Wapello, and so on for dozens of entries. When we are finished with those place names, we will have to rename every single geographic feature that has a name such as "Mesa," "Mountain," "Arroyo," and "Rio." Let's not forget to change the words "ranch," "mosquito," "rodeo," "coyote," "bronco," "vista," and that beautiful vegetable the Aztecs gave us, "tomato."

My favorite Old World term is "loco," from that infamous weed that made animals behave erratically. Let's keep that word. It works well for anyone who supports an English-only law.

The Shadow Beneath the Mountains
—*Peter McBride*

Just west of Aspen, Colorado, hungry souls line the counter at Taqueria El Nopal. The polka beat of ranchero music, the smell of grease, and calling-card advertisements fill the small concrete interior. A heavily mustached cook dishes up beef, chicken, tongue, cheek, and intestine tacos. A typical Monday.

If it were not for the snow-covered mountains outside, which I have known my whole life, I would mistake the place for central Mexico. I am the only Anglo in the restaurant and my less-than-fluent Spanish is obvious. Even the sodas are served in thick glass bottles with "Producto de México" marked on the labels.

Five years ago, the same grill cooked up your typical greasy-spoon burger and fries. It was the Charburger, a favorite among those from the hourly wage working class who came to the valley to be ski bums in the winter.

Today, high prices and a lack of affordable housing in and around the resort of Aspen have caused the raccoon-eyed ski-bum crowd to dwindle, and places like the Charburger have changed.

Unlike the majority of restaurants in the area, the quaint taqueria is not a pricey Mexican-theme joint for tourists. It is a taste of home for the valley's new Latino labor force, who maintain a low profile behind the curtain of Aspen's high-end resort stage.

Silvia Barbera, director of Asistencia Para Latinos, a nonprofit organization established to aid Latino residents, estimates that the number of legal and illegal immigrants has boomed to some 14,000 people, making up almost one-fourth of the population in the forty-five-mile corridor between Aspen and Glenwood. The majority, who come mostly from Texas's southern neighbor, the state of Chihuahua, Mexico, speak little or no English, and only a few have gone past a high school education.

Most are eager to work one or two or even more jobs, live in cramped quarters, and commute long hours to Aspen. Such a lifestyle is not desirable to the ski bum anymore. So with a Mexican economy unable to keep pace with its growing population, Mexicans have become the worker bees who make the beds, bag the groceries, and chop the veggies in Aspen's fine restaurants.

Ironically, while Aspen boasts a world-class experience, most of these new Latino workers will tell you they wouldn't dream of living here as "real" residents or even vacationing here, and few, if any, like skiing.

Take Abisai Olave, who has made Aspen his legal second home for sixteen years. "I have good bosses," he says, "but I always return home to Chihuahua. I don't like snow," he says with a smile. More seriously, he tells me, slightly lifting the brim of his cowboy hat, he likes his traditions, music, people, and Mexican food. All Mexico lacks, he says, are good jobs. The wages Abisai earns working manual labor jobs in Aspen are ten times those in Chihuahua.

Abisai's brother Josué used to live and work in the Aspen area, but despite a current green card, he refuses to leave his small agricultural community of Gomez Farias, Mexico. He says he has seen too many families and communities destroyed from chasing dollars in the States.

Another brother, Daniel, is a U.S. citizen who works as the pastor in a Latino church not far from Taqueria El Nopal but hopes to return to Chihuahua permanently, once he saves enough money. "Why? Because I am American but Mexican at heart," says Daniel as he thumps his chest.

While such Latin-blooded patriotism brings a new flavor to our homogeneous valley, it also creates problems. The majority of Latinos come strictly to work, not to create a community, even a temporary one. With no loyalty to a specific community, many, especially the youth, struggle to keep their identity. They cling to what heritage they can, usually their language.

Hiding behind their native tongue results in less interaction between the two communities, and even cases of racially driven gang violence. The transitory state of the Latino community also leads to a lack in leadership. Without Latino representatives, there is little understanding of the valley's new members and the ingredients that prompt violence.

Will Aspen come to grips with its ski-bum replacements? I hope so. Over time, more Latino workers and their children may come to see the United States as home, and some will get the education they need to prosper here.

As prices in Aspen continue to soar and economic conditions in Mexico remain dismal, though, I fear change is unlikely. The new worker bees will continue to be distant and isolated, and Aspen will remain a community divided.

Views from the Underground
—*Paul Larmer*

"I don't know what we're going to do if the mine closes." The woman's voice sounds strained and tired through the phone. "I'm going to have to find a job, and we may have to cash in our retirement fund. I guess we'll move if we have to."

I hadn't meant to pry. I had just called to remind her of her daughter's peewee basketball practice that night, but in a small western town you can't help but run into the lives of your neighbors.

Like everyone else in town, I had heard about the fire in one of the underground coal mines, about the high levels of carbon monoxide that forced an emergency evacuation. I knew people were worried the company might shut down its operation permanently, putting the top breadwinner in more than a hundred families out of work. That voice made it real. It suddenly registered that nearly half the girls on my team had parents who worked in one of the three local mines.

I'm a slow learner, but I have my excuses. I moved here seven years ago, fresh off a stint with the Sierra Club, the nation's largest environmental group, based in San Francisco, California. There, I was one of dozens of people working feverishly to protect the country's air, water, and last wild places. We rarely discussed the people who worked the land and lived in small rural towns, and when we did it was not in flattering terms. We also talked a language of superlatives: Old trees were "ancient forests"; the Arctic National Wildlife Refuge, under threat of oil drilling, was the "American Serengeti"; and the forces aligned against our last wilderness areas were all big:—Big Oil, Big Timber, and Big Mining just chomping at the bit to plunder the public lands.

Of course there was a kernel of truth in our words. Corporations and wealthy industrialists have frequently and continuously grabbed for resources in the West with little regard for the health of the environment. The landscape in places has been irrevocably changed for the worse. And opportunists are still out there scheming new ways to make a profit off the public domain, though today the ski and off-road-vehicle industries—Big Recreation, if you will—seem more a threat than the traditional bogeymen.

The world of environmental politics left me feeling disconnected from community, which is one reason I left the city and moved to this small town. Still, I was a little apprehensive about settling in a coal mining town. Those miners were "Big Tough Guys" who probably chewed up environmentalists for dinner.

Reality, of course, is more interesting than fiction. The first miner I met was my neighbor Bob, a tall, affable, sandy-haired father of two. Within a week we were chatting regularly over the fence about gardening, fishing holes, and the weather. He gave us some of his garlic crop; we gave him a young apple tree we didn't know what to do with. Then there was Louis, the retired mine electrician who could talk you under the table about everything from how life has gone to hell since the unions left the valley to "those damn kids"who race their pickups down the alley between our houses. Under his feisty exterior, Louis has a warm heart. On more than one cold winter's night, he has fixed our aging coal furnace.

Not all coal miners are sweetness and light, of course. Some are rough and violent. Coal mining is a difficult occupation, even in these modern times. Twelve-hour shifts, six days a week, can take a toll on miner and family. Miners also fear constantly about their jobs. I caught a glimpse of this two years ago on a tour of another coal mine owned then by the giant Arco mining company. We drove deep into the blackness of the mountain until we came to the massive longwall machinery. There a great blade shaved chunks of glistening coal onto a belt that ran like a swollen, lumpy river out of the mountain to the railroad tracks.

Someone asked about the company's commitment to the local community. "Oh, we're not going anywhere," said the mine engineer. "We've got another twenty years' worth of coal down there, at least."

"This is one of the most productive underground coal mines in the country," the company executive seconded.

The next morning, a small story in *The Denver Post* announced that Arco had just put all of its North American coal-mine operations up for sale. So much for stability.

Those miners kept their jobs because the new owners didn't significantly change the mine's operation. It could have been hit-the-road time for the families of the fire-stricken coal mine, just as it might be later this year should the owners decide to cut their losses.

Life isn't black and white in the rural West. You can like miners and dislike the dangerous and capricious nature of their business, just as you can want to protect the environment but still value mining and agricultural communities over exclusive ski-resort towns.

The week of the mine fire a few more fathers brought their girls to practice, including the husband of the woman I called on the phone. He seemed in good spirits and stayed for a while to shoot hoops with his daughter. I hope he's back working underground soon.

Fenced in by the Open Range Law
—Kim Vacariu

I've never liked fences. I've always thought they put man's selfish mark on the landscape and unacceptably hindered wildlife.

So when I was faced with putting barbed wire around my forty acres in southeastern Arizona, I thought long and hard. I knew that a fence would cause the mule deer to detour around the property. Worse, I cringed at the thought of a bulldozer tearing through fragile, high-desert vegetation to cut a fence line.

Yet I went ahead with the project.

It wasn't pleasant. When I inspected the newly cleared fence line, I winced at the sight of several ancient, uprooted mesquite trees.

It wasn't cheap, either. The project took four miles of barbed wire, several pickup loads of metal stakes and stays, and about six months' worth of labor. The final bill for the job was more than $4,000—no small pittance for someone on my budget.

The casual observer might wonder why someone who dislikes fences would put himself through such a project. The truth is I was forced into it, and despite the drawbacks, I admit that I actually felt a sense of satisfaction as I helped tie the final wire that sealed off the property from the rest of the surrounding land. Why? From that moment on, there would never be another cow on my property.

Cows had been grazing the sacaton and blue grama grasses on my acreage for at least a century, and there was very little of it left. I figured cows had been knocking down prickly pear and cholla, chewing wildflowers into extinction, since right after Geronimo last rode through. In fact, cows had been polluting the little seasonal creek, trampling its fragile banks to dust, chewing back the cottonwood sprouts, and dropping noxious weed seeds, since before this land was even in the United States.

All that ended with the final twist of my fencing pliers. I had complied, reluctantly, with the ageless "open range" law of the West, which mandates a rancher's right to graze cattle on any rural property that isn't fenced.

It made me a little nervous, to tell you the truth. The owner of the evicted cows would surely not take kindly to the news that he had just lost a sizable chunk of free grazing land. However, I rationalized that the sparse riparian vegetation left along the creek couldn't possibly have put much meat on any of the twenty or thirty head that usually grazed there.

My fencing dilemma, like that of many rural property owners in the West, has long been overshadowed by the loud debate over grazing on public lands, but the issues are largely the same. In many states, such as Arizona and New Mexico, the "open range" rule is statutory law, allowing ranchers a controversial perk that is being questioned more and more as private rangelands are subdivided and sold off.

Under the law, owners of large tracts can split up their ranches, collect profits on the sale of lots, and then continue to reap the benefits of free grazing on the same parcels. Even if fences are established, they must be maintained. If a fence breaks (or mysteriously comes down) and cows get in, it is the property owner's problem, not the rancher's.

Whether this nineteenth-century law can survive in the growing suburban society of the New West remains to be seen. No one wants cattle ranching to disappear from the culture of the West—an eventuality ranchers claim is imminent if the open range is no longer. Yet as a modern population struggles to adapt to the challenges of making a living in tight urban times, so must those who make their livings in tight agricultural times.

In the meantime the small cottonwoods along the creek, which had struggled against all odds, now have leaders protruding from their trampled stubble. Last fall the grasses inside my fence went to seed for the first time in who knows how long. The wildflowers, thanks to El Niño, have been something to see. The stubs of cholla and prickly pear are showing new growth, blossoming profusely in beautiful yellows and whites. If I didn't know any better, I'd swear I can hear the landscape breathing a sigh of relief.

Confessions of a Recreation Junkie

—Colin Chisholm

For most of my life, I've been an adrenaline junkie. I've road-tripped thousands of gas-guzzling miles to ski peaks, mountain-bike slickrock, climb granite towers, and kayak rivers. I've bolted and jolted, treaded and shredded, pedaled and paddled my way around the West.

All the while mightily wagging my bird finger at the logging truck roaring by, smugly shaking my head at the open-pit mine's deep gash on the hillside, ranting and raving at the dung-dripping bovines trampling the cryptogam, seething at those redneck you-know-whats tearing up the turf with their off-road machines.

All safe, of course, within the confines of my SUV, speeding down the highway, window open, Neil Young blasting from the stereo, my bumper stickers saying it all: Save That, Free That, and Just Do It, why don't you? Trying to live the good life, the healthful life, the green life, the life I first saw in the Patagonia catalogue, then lived for a month on an Outward Bound course.

Life is not so easy for me anymore. Maybe it's some acquired wisdom that has come with age, or perhaps my eyes have finally opened to the monster that has been creeping up behind me all these years.

Anyone who has lived in the West for any length of time has seen the phenomenal growth of outdoor recreation. Along with Wal-Mart and Taco Bell, the so-called "fringe sports" have slithered into nearly every western nook and cranny. Who doesn't rock climb, kayak, mountain-bike, or hike anymore? Combine this with the West's population explosion and what we have today is an outdoor-recreation nightmare, the likes of which compares to extractive industry in terms of its real and potential effects on the natural world.

But I sound like a soothsayer. What I mean to say is this: Outdoor recreation is prettily packaged *use*. Be it fishing, spelunking, kayaking, or horse packing, each and every form of outdoor recreation brings with it an impact that is not easily measured. For most forms of outdoor recreation, there are no long-term studies detailing environmental impact; we're just beginning to understand that each new outdoor fad brings with it unforeseen consequences.

Consider, for example, kayakers upsetting the nesting habits of harlequin ducks, climbers disturbing peregrine falcons, and mountain bikers spreading noxious weeds. Many of us environmentalists recognize the evils of ORVs and snowmobiles but accept our own supposedly less impactful pursuits. We decry the activities of miners and loggers as we flock to the vast playgrounds of our public lands.

Fifteen years ago activities such as backpacking were synonymous with environmentalism. When I encountered another of my ilk in the canyons or mountains, I could be fairly sure we shared an environmental ethic. Backpacking or climbing or biking was merely a means by which we gained access to beautiful places. That's not the case anymore. Today, I often run into recreationists who seem to see the landscape only through the lens of their sport. Increasingly the fisherman supports protection of rivers for the fishing rather than the river, and the mountain biker supports public-land protection for the ride, not the health of the land.

Like any true addict, I don't know when and if I'll stop. Probably I'll keep chugging down the petrol in search of that elusive archetype: the wild. Hopefully I'll lessen my impact by recreating closer to home; perhaps I'll even give up kayaking to work in the garden. Maybe I'll stop pointing fingers.

It's time for outdoor recreationists—motorized or not—to acknowledge the impacts we have on the land and to reconsider our motivations. Unless you give up that sweet red Toyota 4Runner, ditch the Synchilla and Gore-Tex, become a hunter-gatherer, and live like a homesteader in an earth-dug home, nothing is black and white anymore.

Of Cathedrals and Petroglyphs
—Susan Tweit

Sitting on a wooden chair in the soaring nave of Notre Dame de Chartres, one of Europe's most treasured medieval cathedrals, I am thinking about petroglyphs. In front of me, cathedral expert Malcolm Miller is telling our attentive group about the cathedral's glory, its original thirteenth-century stained-glass windows, which glow like jewels even in the subdued light of this dark January day.

It is these jewel-like windows, "a medieval library," in Malcolm Miller's words, that remind me of the petroglyphs etched on a windblown volcanic escarpment half a world away, near Albuquerque, New Mexico. Like Chartres' stained-glass windows, the more than 15,000 petroglyphs protected within Petroglyph National Monument are the pictorial record of a people's spiritual and cultural beliefs.

Also like the windows at Chartres' Gothic cathedral, these images in stone record truths still worshipped and taught today. "The Petroglyph National Monument area is a sacred place," says Bill Weahkee, representing the five Sandoval Indian pueblos. "It is recognized by all the pueblos." The whole escarpment of West Mesa, he explains, is a place of ritual and prayer, a shrine to Pueblo spiritual and cultural heritage. Pueblo people come to this mesa edge to pray and perform sacred rituals, much as modern-day worshippers attend masses at Notre Dame de Chartres.

Unlike the windows at Chartres Cathedral, the petroglyphs along West Mesa above Albuquerque are endangered by development. In 1990, Congress established Petroglyph National Monument to preserve in perpetuity the lively human and animal figures, intricate masks, and careful geometric designs chiseled through the dark desert varnish on the rocks.

Perpetuity, in this case, however, may be short-lived. The monument's 7,200 acres, part of which string like a necklace along the rim of West Mesa, stand between the explosive suburban growth on the western side of Albuquerque and undeveloped prairie beyond. In order to reduce traffic congestion on the west side, the City of Albuquerque wants to "extend" (read "blast a six-lane freeway-type road") a highway through the monument and its petroglyphs.

The proposed road extension has been controversial from the start. Two different polls conducted for Friends of the Petroglyphs, a nonprofit organization fighting the road, show that two-thirds of registered voters in Bernalillo County oppose the road extension and would, in fact, pay more for routes avoiding the monument. Still, the City of Albuquerque has moved forward.

Last fall, New Mexico Senator Pete Domenici (R) and Representative Steve Schiff (R) introduced bills into Congress to delete 8.5 acres of the petroglyph escarpment "as if never included in the Monument." Congress will vote on the Petroglyph National Monument Boundary Adjustment Act sometime this spring. If passed, the act will slice the monument and its sacred spaces in two.

Why is it, I wonder as I watch a moment of fitful January sun pour through the stained-glass windows high overhead at Chartres, that we can so easily perceive the importance of this Gothic cathedral yet fail to see the same sacred qualities in the West Mesa petroglyphs? Imagine the French government proposing to slice through Chartres Cathedral to improve traffic flow. Ludicrous. What blindness afflicts our vision of Petroglyph National Monument?

I am a Quaker, part of a religious tradition that embraces simplicity in religious practices and in our lives. Quakers worship in plain "meeting houses" rather than churches and would no more build elaborate cathedrals than carve fantastic petroglyphs. Yet I can respect the faith that inspires spiritual traditions different from my own. More than that, my Quakerism is enriched and deepened by contact with the sacred places and practices of other cultures and religions. As threads in the diverse human experience, Chartres Cathedral and the petroglyphs of Petroglyph National Monument are equally part of the spiritual inheritance of all human beings, no matter what our backgrounds.

I am reminded of a sign in the Cathedral of Saint Francis in Santa Fe: "This is a sacred place. Please behave accordingly." I want to inscribe those words in huge letters in the blue sky above the escarpment of West Mesa, over Petroglyph National Monument, for all to see and heed.

Contributors

JOHN ADAMS works for the Montana Wilderness Association. He completed his master's thesis in 1998 on the appropriate role of off-road vehicles in national forests. He lives in Missoula, Montana.

BRUCE BABBITT is the former governor of Arizona and the Secretary of the U.S. Department of the Interior.

ROCKY BARKER is the author of *Saving All the Parts: Reconciling Economics and the Endangered Species Act*. He is a founder of the Writers on the Range News Service and the environmental reporter for the *Idaho Statesman*.

ANDREA BARNETT is a freelance journalist who covers Montana politics and environmental issues. Her work has appeared in *High Country News, Mother Jones* magazine, *Missoula Independent, Billings Outpost,* and *Bozeman Tributary.*

CODY BEERS works for the Wyoming Game and Fish Department. He is an avid hunter and angler and lives in Cheyenne, Wyoming.

LOU BENDRICK's work has appeared in such publications as *Dog & Kennel, Ski* magazine, and *Outside*. A former columnist for *The Aspen Times* in Aspen, Colorado, she currently lives in Telluride, Colorado.

ASTA BOWEN is the author of *Hungry for Home: A Wolf Odyssey* and *The Huckleberry Book*. Her op-ed column has run regularly in the *Seattle Post-Intelligencer* since 1988. She lives and writes in a converted Tannery near Flathead Lake in Montana.

KARL BROOKS recently joined the University of Kansas as assistant professor of environmental history and policy. After graduating from Harvard Law School, he practiced law and served three terms in the Idaho Senate.

COLIN CHISHOLM's work has appeared in many magazines and anthologies. His first book is entitled *Through Yup'ik Eyes*. He divides his time between Missoula, Montana, and Prescott, Arizona.

An independent business writer, journalist and essayist, JOHN CLAYTON also teaches advanced writing courses at Rocky Mountain College in Billings, Montana. He is the author of *Small Town Bound*.

HAL CLIFFORD is the author of *The Falling Season: Inside the Life & Death Drama of Aspen's Mountain Rescue Team*. He has written for *The New York Times Magazine, The Wall Street Journal,* and *Outside*, and is a regular contributor to *National Geographic Adventure* and *High Country News*. He lives in Telluride, Colorado.

STEVE COLLECTOR's photographs have been exhibited widely. He freelances for numerous magazines and periodicals, including *Esquire, Men's Journal, Outside,* and *High Country News.* He is the author of the award-winning book *Law of the Range: Portraits of Old-Time Brand Inspectors.*

DAN DAGGET is the author of *Beyond the Rangeland Conflict: Toward a West that Works.* He consults with ranchers wanting to practice sustainable management of their land. He lives in Flagstaff, Arizona.

WILLIAM DEBUYS' latest book is *Salt Dreams: Land and Water in Low-Down California.* He lives in Santa Fe, New Mexico, and works for the Conservation Fund.

BRAD DIMOCK spent more than 25 years as a river guide in the Grand Canyon and around the world. He is co-author of *The Doing of the Thing,* the award-winning biography of Buzz Holmstrom. His latest book is titled *Sweep Scow: The Search for Glen & Bessie Hyde.*

JIM DWYER lives and writes in Bisbee, Arizona.

TIMOTHY EGAN, a national correspondent for *The New York Times,* is the author of *Lasso the Wind: Away to the New West.*

SUSAN EWING's latest book is *The Great Rocky Mountain Nature Factbook.* She co-edited the anthology *Shadow Cat: Encountering the American Mountain Lion.*

DAVID FEEL teaches at Montezuma-Cortez High School in Cortez, Colorado, and writes a monthly column for *Inside/Outside* magazine.

CHRIS FRASIER, a fifth-generation High Plains rancher, lives near Limon, Colorado. Writing, especially about natural resource issues, is an avocation that "helps fill the time between waking up and having breakfast."

A performance poet, freelance writer, and Green Party member, ART GOODTIMES is a county commissioner on Colorado's western slope and a grower of heirloom seed potatoes.

DAVID GOWDEY lives and writes in Williams, Arizona.

LINDA HASSELSTROM is a rancher and author of many books, poems, and articles on life in the West. She lives in South Dakota.

MARTY JONES plays music and writes columns for *Westword,* an alternative newspaper in Denver, Colorado.

DAN KEMMIS is the former mayor of Missoula, Montana, and the author of *Community and The Politics of Place.* He directs the Center for the Rocky Mountain West in Missoula, Montana.

PAUL KRZA is a Rock Springs, Wyoming, native who has worked for 30 years as a radio and print journalist. His work has appeared most recently in

Denver and Albuquerque. He currently lives in Socorro, New Mexico.

PAUL LARMER is the senior editor of *High Country News* and the editor of the paper's syndicated columns service, Writers on the Range.

DEWEY LINZE is a veteran journalist who has spent much of his career with the *Los Angeles Times*. He now lives in Gardnerville, Nevada.

STEPHEN LYONS is the author of *Landscape of the Heart*, a single father's memoir. A native of Chicago's south side, Lyons moved to the West in 1973.

RICHARD MANNING is the author of four books, including *One Round River: The Curse of Gold and the Fight for the Big Blackfoot*. He now freelances for *Harper's*, the *Los Angeles Times*, *The New York Times*, *Audubon*, *High Country News*, and other publications. He lives in Lolo, Montana.

ED MARSTON is a former New York physics professor turned western journalist. He is the publisher of *High Country News*, which has covered the communities and environment of the American West for 30 years.

MARK MATTHEWS, from Missoula, Montana, works as regular correspondent for *The Washington Post*, *High Country News*, *Great Falls Tribune*, and *Wildland Firefighter*. His first book, *Peace Jumpers*, chronicles the history of World War II conscientious objectors who helped transform an experimental smoke-jumper program into the elite fire-fighting force of the U.S. Forest Service.

PETER MCBRIDE is a freelance journalist and photographer whose work has appeared in *National Geographic* and *High Country News*. He lives in Aspen, Colorado.

MERVIN MECKLENBURG is managing editor of *The Ranger-Review* in Glendive, Montana.

After a career in ski and tourism promotion, MARK MENLOVE "dropped out" to pursue a graduate degree in creative writing at the University of Arizona in Tucson. He is a frequent contributor to *Lodestar* magazine, and his work was included in the anthology *Park City Witness*.

CHINLE MILLER lives in both Montrose, Colorado, and Moab, Utah, working as an archaeologist and writer. Her forthcoming book, *Desert Rats*, is a portrait of people who love the American desert Southwest.

CHRISTINA NEALSON is author of *Living on the Spine*. Her latest book of nonfiction is *Menopause, Nature and the Unlived Soul*. She lives in Taos, New Mexico.

MICHELLE NIJHUIS is the associate editor of *High Country News*. She lives in Paonia, Colorado.

DAN OKO is a freelance journalist and former editor of *The Missoula Independent* in Missoula, Montana. He currently lives in Austin, Texas.

DON OLSEN lives in Hotchkiss, Colorado, where he publishes *The Valley Chronicle* and attempts to build a solar house.

DAVID PETERSEN writes full-time from his handmade cabin in the San Juan Mountains of southwest Colorado. He is the author of nine books, including, most recently, *Heartsblood: Hunting, Spirituality, and Wildness in America*.

CHARLES PEZESHKI is an author and environmental activist based in Pullman, Moscow. In his spare time he teaches mechanical engineering at the University of Idaho.

ED QUILLEN is the publisher of *Colorado Central* magazine in Salida, Colorado, a columnist for *The Denver Post*, and the author of *Deep in the Heart of the Rockies*.

TOM REED lives and works in the shadow of the Wind River Mountains outside Lander, Wyoming, with a string of saddle horses and an English setter named Hank. When he's not writing, he's in the wilderness teaching courses for the National Outdoor Leadership School.

PENELOPE REEDY is a reporter for the *Idaho State Journal* and an English instructor at Idaho State University. From 1975 to 1995, she edited and published *The Redneck Review of Literature*, a magazine of contemporary western American literature and culture. She lives in Pocatello, Idaho.

RAY RING is a novelist and journalist based in Bozeman, Montana. He has worked for the *Arizona Daily Star* and *High Country News* and is currently a managing editor with the *Bozeman Chronicle*.

MICHAEL ROBINSON works for the Center for Biological Diversity in Pinos Altos, New Mexico. He is writing a book about the politics and cultural history of the federal wolf extermination campaign.

JOHN ROSAPEPE has written about baseball, grizzlies, Lewis and Clark, salmon and Shakespeare in the West. These days he can be found sea kayaking in the Chesapeake Bay and Puget Sound.

AUDEN SCHENDLER is environmental manager at Aspen Skiing Company. Previously a research associate on corporate sustainability at the Rocky Mountain Institute, he has been a high school teacher, trailer insulator, and Outward Bound instructor. He lives in Carbondale, Colorado.

MARY SOJOURNER, under the influence of Edward Abbey, came

West in 1985 to write and fight for what's left of this land. She has written novels, short stories, and essays, and is a commentator for National Public Radio.

JIM STILES is a former park ranger and the editor and publisher of *The Canyon Country Zephyr*, an alternative publication out of Moab, Utah.

STEPHEN STUEBNER is a freelance writer who covers natural resources, politics, and the outdoors for a wide range of publications. He lives in Boise, Idaho.

A field ecologist who "evolved" into a writer, SUSAN J. TWEIT is an award-winning author and radio commentator who writes for such magazines as *Audubon* and *Cricket*. Her latest book is *Seasons on the Pacific Coast: A Naturalist's Notebook*. She lives in Salida, Colorado.

KIM VACARIU is a journalist who lives and writes in Tucson, Arizona.

HAL WALTER is a former newspaper editor and author of *Pack Burro Stories*. He makes his home in the central Colorado region.

Raised in the logging country of northern California, LOUISE WAGENKNECHT now writes from Idaho, where she ponders the ways of the New West among a small flock of sheep. Her essays have appeared in *American Nature Writing 1999* and *Ring of Fire: Writers of the Yellowstone Region*.

NORM WALLEN arrived in Flagstaff, Arizona, in 1993 after retiring from San Francisco State University, where he was professor of educational psychology. He is a member of the Flagstaff City Council, the executive committee of the Grand Canyon Chapter of the Sierra Club, and the Diablo Trust land-management team.

DAN WHIPPLE is a freelance writer now living in Colorado. He served as editor of *High Country News* during the dark ages and now specializes in writing about science and environmental issues.

PAT WILLIAMS represented Montana in the U.S. House of Representatives for 18 years and now works at the University of Montana's Center for the Rocky Mountain West in Missoula.

KEN WRIGHT is a writer, river guide, and father living in Durango, Colorado. His first book is *A Wilder Life: Essays from Home*. His pieces from this collection will appear in his second book, *Travels of a Pleistocene Man: An Ancient Defense of the Modern West*.

SUSAN ZAKIN is the author of *Coyotes and Town Dogs: Earth First! and the Environmental Movement*. She lives in Tucson, Arizona.

Index